Mustang Ride

Riding our Mustangs through
herds of bison in Yellowstone
National Park, Wyoming.

Mustang Ride

THE ADVENTURES OF THE WILSON sisters in the American West

KELLY WILSON

RANDOM HOUSE
NEW ZEALAND

This book is dedicated to Alexa and Kirsty, two of the most beautiful souls we've had the pleasure of knowing. Thank you for joining us on our Mustang adventure, it wouldn't have been the same without you; also to the special people we met during our travels across the Wild West and who helped make our time in the USA some of the best months of our lives.

RANDOM HOUSE

UK | USA | Canada | Ireland | Australia
India | New Zealand | South Africa | China

Random House is an imprint of the Penguin Random House group of companies, whose addresses can be found at global.penguinrandomhouse.com

 Penguin
Random House
New Zealand

First published by Penguin Random House New Zealand, 2016

10 9 8 7 6 5 4 3 2 1

Text © Kelly Wilson, 2016

Images © Kelly Wilson, Amanda Wilson and Kirsty Wagstaff, 2016

The moral right of the author has been asserted.

Design by Sam Bunny © Penguin Random House New Zealand
Cover images: Kelly Wilson and Paige Barnett
Back cover: The view from our cabin in Wyoming, where we were based for the majority of our first month in America's Wild West.
Prepress by Image Centre Group
Printed and bound in China by Leo Paper Products Ltd

A catalogue record for this book is available from the National Library of New Zealand.

ISBN 978-0-14-377016-9
eISBN 978-0-14-377017-6

penguin.co.nz

CONTENTS

A wild Mustang foal in the Pryor Mountains of Montana.

Prologue

Amanda and Showtym Cassanova jumping in the
2016 Olympic Cup where they placed second,
winning enough prize money to buy her Mustang,
Bragg, a plane ticket home to New Zealand.

I watched with pride as my younger sister, Amanda, guided her pinto showjumper around the course in the second round of the Olympic Cup, the most prestigious showjumping class in New Zealand. Showtym Cassanova was one of only seven horses that had jumped clear in the opening round, and the pressure and expectations were daunting. Only the very best combinations competed in the Olympic Cup, with many riders flying in from Australia to compete for the coveted prize. So far only one other horse had jumped a double clear round, the Polish import Carnutelabryere ridden by English rider Helen McNaught-McFarlane who had recently relocated to New Zealand.

As Amanda approached the sixth fence, her face showed a combination of steely determination and ease — although she was aware of the difficulty of the course, she was sure that her horse was capable, and indeed they flew over the oxer before continuing on to the double, leaving all of the rails up. From there they rolled back to an upright set at 1.57 metres and cantered down to the perfect spot, jumping effortlessly. Soon the final jump was behind them, and with a huge grin Amanda leant forward to give Cassanova a pat.

As she left the ring our older sister Vicki met her at the gate, giving Cassanova a handful of feed before smiling up at Amanda, congratulating her on a perfectly ridden round; there hadn't been a thing to fault. I pushed through the crowd, eager to join them, and gave Amanda a hug before reaching down to remove Cassanova's boots. There were only a few minutes before he would be back in the arena for the third and final round, and it was important that he was refreshed.

The final horse left the arena, having knocked a rail down, and the announcer called the draw for the jump-off. Helen would ride first, and Amanda would be second and last — only two riders had qualified.

Carnutelabryere set a good time, jumping clear, and Amanda was both excited and nervous as she stood at the gate. She was guaranteed to place second, regardless of how she did in the ring, so with nothing to lose she and Vicki had carefully outlined a path that would shave valuable seconds off the clock, hopefully ensuring the win.

Entering the arena, she checked that everything was in place and settled

Cassanova into a canter, waiting for the bell before she approached the first fence, jumping it easily. Approaching the second fence, an imposing brick wall, she miscalculated the distance; Cassanova gallantly tried to correct his stride, clearing the jump but knocking a brick down. With four faults they were now in second position, and Amanda jumped the next fence with ease before circling and coming back to a walk, nodding to the judges to indicate that she was retiring.

After congratulating Helen for her superb performance, she rode over to join Vicki and me, unable to stop grinning. Although the jump-off hadn't gone to plan, she'd ridden to win and had no regrets. Even better, she'd finished second in the Olympic Cup and was incredibly proud of her horse; it was a huge achievement.

Side by side, Helen and Amanda rode into the arena in front of thousands of onlookers for the prize-giving. As Cassanova's blue ribbon was tied to his neck, Amanda suddenly thought of another horse that had come to mean just as much to her as Cassanova — her wild American Mustang, Bragg. She knew exactly what she wanted to spent the $25,000 of prize money on.

As Amanda cantered out of the arena to the song 'Stand Up for the Champions', her excitement continued to build. Cassanova had made not one but two of her dreams come true — placing in the Olympic Cup for their second consecutive year, and the chance of being reunited with Bragg, who she'd had to leave behind in in America just a few months before.

Amanda drew Cassanova to a halt beside us, and announced that she was spending her prize money on flying her Mustang home.

Introduction

Two wild Mustang stallions fighting at sunset in the Pryor Mountains of Montana.

I grew up with my older and younger sisters, Vicki and Amanda, in New Zealand's Northland. From the beginning we were all passionate about horses, and still are. Money was always tight, so we often rode bareback and could only afford the cheapest ponies — which often had a reputation for being difficult, but were usually simply misunderstood or injured. We developed training methods based on building love and trust with each horse, allowing them to develop at their own pace rather than being forced, and to learn to enjoy all that life offered. Our parents were always wonderfully supportive and encouraged us to live our dreams.

Showjumping became a big part of our lives, with all of us achieving success in the arena at the highest levels — on horses that jumped well because they wanted to. Sheer hard work and determination enabled us to start Showtym Horses, our family business, where we train young riders and horses alongside our own, building it up to a 25-hectare (65-acre) property with a stable of 50 horses. Training and competing is Vicki's main focus; she is one of the country's most competitive (and successful) riders. Amanda is equally passionate about writing and filming as showjumping; I compete mostly for fun, but my other work — design, photography and writing — has also come to revolve around horses.

It is perhaps unsurprising that we are also involved in taming wild horses. Since 2012, we have become advocates and trainers for New Zealand's wild horses, the Kaimanawas. We are passionate about improving horse welfare worldwide, and about building awareness of just how wonderful wild horses can be.

For all three of us, fictional wild horses were an integral part of our childhood. In a time before computers and the internet were commonplace, we would spend hours reading stories about horses; many of these revolved around the wild Mustangs found in America's Wild West. As our respect for the abilities of our rescued Kaimanawas grew, so too did our interest in the plight of wild horses everywhere. The more we learnt, the more we saw a growing need for someone to champion the cause of these horses, and we took it upon ourselves to research, read and watch everything we could on the wild horses we had first discovered in

Top
A wild Kiger Mustang, recognisable by the zebra-like stripes on the upper legs.

Bottom
Some of the 800 once-wild Mustangs now held in the Delta Wild Horse and Burro Facility in Utah.

the pages of our childhood books all those years ago.

We looked at the situation in other countries. With an estimated 400,000 to 1 million Brumbies running, almost totally unmanaged, in the wild, Australia has a serious problem. An uncontrolled number of horses are being slaughtered every year for meat, aerial culling occurs regularly and the infamous Brumby 'running', where dogs are used to keep the horses running until they are so exhausted they can be caught and roped, means that thousands of these living legends are meeting an undesirable end every year.

After we had helped to drop the slaughter rates of New Zealand's wild Kaimanawas since 2012 (the government musters and culls horses every second year to maintain a herd size of just 300 horses), the countless Brumbies seemed like a daunting and insurmountable problem. While once the majority of the Kaimanawas captured during the government culls were being sent to slaughter, in recent years the attention of mainstream media has been a turning point for these horses: at the 2016 Kaimanawa muster, every horse suitable for re-homing had a family waiting.

In comparison to Australia, the situation in America seemed manageable. Once, two million wild horses had roamed the West, but now only 30,000 can be found on public lands. Each year, excess wild Mustangs and Burros are mustered and — because of an anti-slaughter policy and a lack of people interested in re-homing them — are stockpiled in government holding facilities run by the Bureau of Land Management (BLM). Since 1971, when the United States Congress first recognised Mustangs as 'living symbols of the historic and pioneer spirit of the West', over 270,000 wild horses have been removed from the range despite the outrage of activists. Today, 35 years on, 50,000 wild horses are currently languishing in holding facilities across America, costing taxpayers US$80 million a year to feed and manage. Only a fraction of these are adopted.

In 2007, in a bid to raise public awareness and increase re-homing rates, the Mustang Heritage Foundation (MHF) launched the Extreme Mustang Makeover (EMM), a national training incentive very similar to our own Kaimanawa Stallion Challenges. Since then, over 5000 horses have been saved through this programme — but each year thousands more are captured, and supply continues to outnumber demand. The majority of these captive Mustangs will end their lives in the holding facilities — a far from ideal existence for these once-wild horses. Nothing seems about to change: the musters keep happening, wild Mustangs end up being held captive and good horses are wasting away in prison-like environments.

Even though the Mustangs are a bigger problem than the Kaimanawas, with 50,000 horses in America needing an immediate solution, the huge numbers didn't put us off. Saving a few Mustangs might not change the world in general, but we hoped our journey with them would inspire others to work with Mustangs. So, we got in contact with the MHF to see how we could help. We hoped that we could raise awareness through social media, a book and a documentary, by training Mustangs to become ambassadors for the breed and inspiring others to re-home horses from the BLM yards and offer them a second chance at life.

In early 2015, Vicki, Amanda and I were invited to compete in the Extreme Mustang Makeover. Suddenly our idea about taming America's wild horses seemed like a real possibility and the timing was perfect — the 100 days of training required for the competition started just after the end of the showjumping season and the final leg of the Kaimanawa Stallion Challenges.

With just a few months until we were expected to collect our wild horses on the other side of the world, we decided to commit — despite being in the middle of a busy competition season and still training our Kaimanawa stallions for the Stallion Challenges. Amanda was also the second camerawoman for the television series *Keeping Up With the Kaimanawas*, filming in between training her own Kaimanawa, and I was writing my second book, also about the Stallion Challenges, which the publisher wanted before we left New Zealand. In what little spare time we had, we began finalising passports, applying for visas, booking our flights, finding a ranch to host us and rearranging our lives so that we could be based overseas for the 100 days required to train the wild horses for the competition.

Top
Filming for our television show, *Keeping Up With the Kaimanawas*,
which showcased the plight of New Zealand's wild horses.

Bottom
Vicki's wild Kaimanawa stallion from the 2014 muster, Argo KH, has become a
valued ambassador of the breed and a much loved member of our family.

Our first sighting of the Boise
Bureau of Land Management
yards, just hours after we
arrived in America.

WILD HORSE
CORRALS →

CHAPTER 1

*Cowboy Country,
here we come*

Top
With our luggage at Auckland Airport about to depart for America.

Bottom
It took us a while to feel comfortable working horses in jeans and Western hats but by the time we left America we felt like real cowgirls. From left: Kirsty, Amanda, me, Vicki and Alexa.

Alongside the three of us, two friends were joining us on our American adventure. Although just 18 years old, both Kirsty and Alexa had been riding with us for years, had helped tame wild horses in New Zealand and had also had success in the showjumping arena. While they were happy to come just for the fun of it and tame a Mustang for the memories, we sent an email to the Mustang Heritage Foundation to see if they could also compete in the invitation-only event. They could.

We five would be the only international trainers out of the 38 competing. Deciding to scope out the level of competition, we began watching videos online and our early excitement quickly dissipated. In just 100 days, previous winners of the Extreme Mustang Makeover had their Mustangs performing at a higher level than our Kaimanawa horses were after 150 days! We wondered how wild horses could transition so quickly in such a short period of time — either the level of training and showmanship was far superior to both our own and that of the other New Zealand trainers in the Kaimanawa Stallion Challenges, or the Mustangs weren't as wild as the horses we were used to taming.

We read through the rules of the competition again — and there it was. The underlying difference. The Mustangs used in the competitions were aged from three to seven years and had been in captivity for at least 12 months, to allow the stallions to be gelded and to guarantee that the mares weren't carrying foals. The horses were described as 'virtually unhandled', as opposed to totally untouched. We were left thinking about just what these horses had been through during their time in captivity and how different they would be to the wild Kaimanawas. Not only would these Mustangs be used to fences, eating hay and drinking out of troughs, but they also wouldn't have recently gone through the trauma of a muster. The Kaimanawas we work with in New Zealand arrive on our property in stock trucks the day after they have been mustered by helicopters, the stallions are still entire and the mares are generally carrying foals. On top of that, their age is never guaranteed: we have worked with lead mares as old as 12, and with 18-year-old stallions fresh from the ranges.

With renewed confidence we began looking for a ranch to host us. Since we knew no one near Nampa, Idaho, where the competition was to be, we emailed 50 ranches that take guests — known as 'dude ranches' — within a 10-hour travel-time radius. We sent a detailed proposal of who we were and what we had planned . . . and then the waiting game began. Asking anyone to take on five girls and their wild horses for three months seemed like a huge ask, but to our surprise three ranches were happy to host us. We settled on a ranch in Wyoming; with that finalised, and now only eight weeks until we were due in America, we began some serious organising. Flights were booked, passports renewed and visas applied for. We had a moment of panic when Kirsty's passport was delayed because she wasn't on the register of births — apparently her parents had misspelt her name as 'Kristy' on her birth certificate 18 years earlier. She ended up paying a fortune for an emergency passport and visa in the name of Kristy, and had to change the name on her flights, too, finalising everything with just days to spare.

Meanwhile, we were also caught up in the whirlwind of the competition circuit, competing our team of showjumpers each weekend, and in our spare time training our wild horses for the finals of the Kaimanawa Stallion Challenge at the Horse of the Year show in early March. After the show we would have just two weeks to pack, settle our horses in for the long winter and psychologically prime our parents to look after the 50 horses we were leaving in their care.

THERE WERE TIMES WHEN WE EXPERIENCED MOMENTS of panic, when we realised how little we had actually organised in terms of basing ourselves in America, but in general we didn't have the time to give it much thought. A month out, we realised that we had nowhere to initially train the horses to lead or load, or any way to transport them to the dude ranch 10 hours away and back to the competition at the conclusion of the 100 days of training. A quick email to MHF resulted in a partial solution — another trainer offered the use of his property for the first four days to allow us to get the Mustangs quiet enough to travel, and he also offered to haul our wild horses from the

BLM yards to his property.

Now we just needed to figure out a way to transport the horses to the Wyoming ranch 500 miles away! There were three options: pay a transporter to haul the horses each way, lease a truck and trailer, or buy a truck and trailer. All three seemed like massive financial burdens and overwhelming to organise from the other side of the world. After weeks of trying to phone and email companies we put it in the too-hard basket and decided to wing it once we landed in America — how hard could it be?

To make matters worse, two weeks before we left, Vicki had a fall in the Silver Fern Stakes Grand Prix at the Horse of the Year, dislocating her shoulder. She was the only one of the five of us experienced at driving a truck and trailer with horses, and having been advised that she shouldn't ride for a couple of months, there was a real concern that she wouldn't be able to go to America. However, Vicki decided to go anyway — there would probably be fewer physical demands with only one horse in America than staying behind with 50, as there was no way she would have sat idle if staying in New Zealand over the winter.

With the horse shows behind us and just 12 days until we left, we began last-minute preparations — unshoeing and settling our horses in for the long winter, and ensuring that there was enough hay and feed in the sheds. It was daunting to think we would be gone for over four months, with our time with the Mustangs to be followed by four weeks holiday in Hawaii, Alaska and Canada. To be honest, though, it was a relief to be missing the New Zealand winter, which would have been too quiet for us. Two of the past three winters had been spent taming the Kaimanawas, which are mustered every two years, but with no muster in 2015 and our team of showjumpers on holiday (at the end of the competition season we remove their covers and shoes, and turn them out on the hills in herds to run feral for three months to rest their bodies and give them some mental downtime), we had the freedom and flexibility to base ourselves offshore and were looking forward to doing something new. We were especially pleased to be out of the country when *Keeping Up With the Kaimanawas* was due to air in primetime on the nation's largest broadcasting network. Ratings were expected to be high and we were happy to avoid any resulting media hype.

The only downside was a financial one. The winter months are some of our most profitable: we can increase the client horses we take in for schooling, teach at clinics around the country and host our Showtym Camps. As well as losing all these sources of income, we would be spending money — we were self-funding the entire Mustangs trip and were quickly coming to realise how much it was going to cost.

Packing finally began. We struggled to decide on what to take — there was no way we would fit both normal and horse gear into our suitcases, so rather than pay excess baggage fees we made lists of crucial items to take and items that would be cheaper to purchase in America. As the days sped by, we began to realise how little we had pre-arranged. By nature we are spontaneous, but our lack of planning didn't fully hit us until we stood, exhausted, at Auckland's international airport about to check-in for our flights. We were lucky we'd made it even that far, it had been such a stressful week. At the counter, our excess saddlery made our luggage too heavy, and we began pulling out bridles, halters, boots and winter jackets; a ruthless process that left Amanda with no riding boots, and only two bridles, five bits and three saddles between us — not much for five Kiwi girls about to tame wild horses halfway around the world.

AFTER TWO LAYOVERS AND MORE THAN 30 HOURS of travelling, we landed in Boise, Idaho, at 1 a.m. in the morning — with no place organised to stay. Fighting off exhaustion, we began calling hotels to find a vacancy. It seemed pointless paying for multiple rooms when we had only a few hours of sleep ahead of us, so the five of us crammed into a double queen room and were showered and fast asleep by 3 a.m. Less than four hours later, I was awakened from a deep sleep by our alarm and groggily sat up. After shaking Vicki and Alexa awake, the three of us hurriedly dressed and called a taxi, leaving the other girls to sleep.

We had so much to do before we started working with the wild horses and there was no time to waste. By 8 a.m., we found ourselves standing on the sidewalk on Fairview Avenue, evidently the best place to get a used truck as car dealers graced both sides of the road as far down as the eye could see. At this point, we should point out that our knowledge of vehicles is limited. Although Vicki is used to driving a massive diesel horse truck, her knowledge of maintenance is fairly minimal. Alexa and I were even younger and more naïve when it came to vehicles, and we hoped the car dealers wouldn't pull a fast one on us.

At the first yard we visited it quickly became clear that leasing a truck wasn't an option — meaning that we had to purchase one, something we really hadn't budgeted for. With the exchange rate working against us, we set off to find ourselves the cheapest possible truck that would be up to hauling five horses.

At each yard the guys were helpful; if they didn't have a suitable truck they would call someone in a rival yard, tell them to look after us and send us further down the street. Without fail, when the dealers heard we were in America to tame wild Mustangs, they laughed and looked at us in disbelief; but by the time we finished our story by saying we had only landed in America hours before and needed a truck before lunch-time, they were impressed with our determination and tenacity.

The whole thing was quite a comical experience. By the third dealer, we had gleaned enough information to start sounding savvy and were able to reel off our preferred specifications. Unsurprisingly, we were taken far more seriously when we weren't asking for 'a truck big enough to tow a trailer with five horses' and were able to state that we wanted a diesel, at least a 250HD, fewer than 100,000 miles on it and preferably one of three preferred brands. Not that these things meant anything to us — we were just repeating what the other dealers had recommended would be most suited to our needs.

Soon we had narrowed it down to three trucks, but only one dealer was prepared to give us a buy-back guarantee — by the sounds of it, this wasn't standard practice in America, but it gave us some security; it would be far easier to drop our truck off at the dealer's and collect a cheque than have to find a private buyer in a hurry before flying out of the country. With paperwork and insurance quickly sorted out, soon we were driving our new truck down the road, arriving at the hotel to

TOP
A curious yearling Mustang walks up to be touched in the Boise Wild Horse Corrals.

BOTTOM
Our first sight of the Extreme Mustang Makeover mares in the short-term BLM yards in Boise, Idaho. The black mare from Jackies Butte would later be assigned to me and named Jackie.

pick up Amanda and Kirsty just before check-out time. We were quite pleased with what we'd managed to accomplish since we'd walked off the plane 12 hours earlier.

Our next mission was to find the BLM yards; we'd rung ahead that morning and asked to visit the Mustangs. Although we couldn't collect our horses for another 48 hours, we wanted to see the Mustangs that had been drafted to compete, and get an idea of what the government holding facilities were like; we'd heard and seen plenty of negative media surrounding the highly controversial management of wild horses in America, but were interested to form our own opinions.

Soon we were pulling into the Wild Horse Corrals, where we were met by Steve, the manager. The yards at Boise were only a short-term holding facility with just 100 horses in a few acres; some of the larger yards keep thousands of horses long-term. Quickly making our way to the towering fences, we glanced through at the young horses inside. The first pen was assigned to three- and four-year-old geldings, and a couple wandered towards us to investigate. They stopped a few metres away, but gradually a couple worked up courage and crept closer; when we moved, they spun around in fright and cantered back to the group. A couple snaked their necks, biting and play-fighting. Although clearly bored, these horses were in excellent condition and appeared quite happy with life.

Wandering on, we passed pens filled with juveniles, many pintos and duns; the older horses were predominantly plain colours. The young horses were even more friendly, a few walking right up to the fence line and letting us touch them. Many of them had known no other life, having been born in the BLM yards after their mothers were mustered, and for them confinement and humans were commonplace — many were as friendly as our performance-bred foals in New Zealand.

Moving on, we approached the yards where the Extreme Mustang Makeover mares were contained and immediately sensed the difference — these mares were sorted into groups of six and held in smaller yards, and they were stressed. We paused in front of the first yard and watched a large black mare panicking, pacing back and forth and biting the other horses — she was obviously worried and taking it out on everyone else. Steve explained that the mares chosen for the competition had come from the Burns yards, in Oregon, and had arrived only 10 days earlier. It was the first time they had been transported since they had been gathered from the wild, and it was quite an unsettling time for them.

We spent some time observing the competition Mustangs. Most were nice types and all were solid-coloured. Soon we had three favourites picked out: a beautiful light bay with kind eyes, a chestnut with plenty of white, and a dark bay. All three were quiet and relaxed with excellent conformation — we hoped we would be assigned one of these. The challenge horses were spread between five yards, and in each yard there were varying temperaments. Those in the first and fourth yards were on-edge and overly reactive, but the others seemed calm and stood quietly watching us with interest. Two horses even stepped forward and ate hay from our outstretched fingers.

In an attempt to even the playing field, all of the horses assigned to compete in this year's Idaho Extreme Mustang Makeover were mares aged four to six years, but there were still so many variables. So much of each trainer's success would come down to the mare's temperament and how willing she was to adapt to the many changes ahead of her.

Each horse was branded on the neck, and also had a tag around the neck with a number to help with identification. We asked Steve if we were allowed to find out which horses we had been assigned, and he nodded — he'd tell us which five were ours, but not which horse each of us had individually been assigned. Armed with a list of five numbers, we went back to the yards to check out the tags and soon knew just what we were in for — one of us had the stressed black from the first yard. Two of our favourite three horses were also assigned to us; the last two were also black, one of which had a poor top line (a lack of muscle condition over the horse's body) and short, stilted (upright) hooves that concerned Vicki.

NIGHT WAS NOW FAST APPROACHING, so we returned to the truck and headed west to the property that was hosting us for the Mustangs'

TOP
The Extreme Mustang
Makeover mares from
the first pen were
the most stressed.

MIDDLE
Of the 40 mares selected
for the Extreme Mustang
Makeover, this chestnut
mare from Coyote Lake
was one of our favourites.
She was later assigned to
Alexa and named Coyote.

BOTTOM
Another of our favourites
was this bay mare from
Sand Springs, who was later
paired up with Amanda
and named Spring.

initial handling. From the moment we arrived we felt welcome, and settled down to some serious talking. Matt and Stacie, our hosts, were very generous in sharing their knowledge, keeping us entertained for hours with stories. Matt, who had won the Extreme Mustang Makeover twice, filled us in on how the competition worked.

Three things stood out. First, you had the option to have your horses haltered by the BLM, which he strongly recommended. Second, the Extreme Mustang Makeover horses were generally the Mustangs least likely to be adopted, which was why most were plain-coloured; they were also from less desirable herd management areas, or more likely to be highly strung. Third, and most profound, was Matt's theory on the difference between New Zealand's wild horses, which have no predators, and the wild Mustangs, which are highly sensitised to attacks from coyotes, wolves, snakes and other predators. This, in his opinion, made them more difficult to tame and very unpredictable when ridden. It was certainly something we hadn't considered, and we would definitely keep it in mind when working with our wild ones.

The next day we woke early and spent the morning setting up the yards where our horses would be staying. Although the property was brilliant for working with wild horses, many of the facilities we had at home were missing and we knew we would have to adapt our training methods. But there was no point worrying about it; and in fact, having to work outside our comfort zone was bound to teach us something new — it was guaranteed to be a good learning experience.

That afternoon we went to see a few horse trailers, but none of them was quite what we were looking for. Most were narrow four-horse trailers with small storage areas at the front; five-horse trailers seemed hard to come by. With the dividers removed, and the Mustangs all being pony-sized, we could probably fit five into the four-horse trailers, but it certainly wasn't ideal. We continued our search, and the next day found a stock trailer that would easily fit five wild horses. It had no accommodation or dividers, but was sturdy, wide and, most importantly, within our budget. The owners also agreed to give us a buy-back guarantee for just US$1000 less than we paid for it, assuming that it was returned in the same condition. The trailer still needed some repairs and new tyres but would be ready to collect in a few days, just in time for us to drive the horses east to Wyoming.

That night we returned to Matt's, and three other trainers also joined us — 10 of the 38 people competing would be based here for the first four days of handling, and we were interested to meet everyone and work alongside them; we were sure we could learn a lot from seeing the different training methods. Interestingly, the five of us were the only English-style trainers in the competition, with everyone else having a Western focus; we were quite the novelty. Even a random stranger — an old rancher — who we met at a petrol station laughed when he heard we were in America to tame wild Mustangs. Still chuckling, he said 'Don't get hurt, little ladies' — apparently we were too young, too pretty and too female to be 'broncing out wild horses'.

CHAPTER 2

So it begins

The five wild Mustangs initially drafted to us. Vicki's black mare (middle) was soon vetted out and replaced with a bay mare.

TOP
Vicki with the BLM representatives and vet as they watch her assigned Mustang trotting (middle). The Mustang was soon deemed unsuited for the competition due to hoof and back issues and another mare was bought forward to replace her.

BOTTOM
Alexa's mare being haltered by BLM staff in the padded squeeze crush.

We arrived at the BLM yards early on our third day in America, and the sorting and loading process soon began. Our first priority was to find out which of us had which horse: Vicki was assigned the horse with the back and feet issues, I had the wild black, Amanda had the pretty bay we liked, Alexa had our favourite chestnut and Kirsty had the smallest black mare.

Since Vicki's assigned Mustang had worried her two days before, she set off to the yards to observe the horse before it was drafted forward — we'd had horses with similar damage to their backs and feet in New Zealand and they had required time and extensive rehabilitation; even then, some never recovered enough for ridden work. Each trainer was allowed to swap out their Mustang once within 30 days, if for some reason the horse was unsound or unsuited to ridden work; and if there were problems Vicki would rather be reassigned a horse now, since we were going to be based so far away. After her closer observation Vicki felt that both of the issues, although not necessarily permanent, made the horse unsuitable for the intensive training required for the 100-day challenge, and the BLM and vets agreed. She was reassigned a second horse; a narrow bay was sorted out from the yard full of spares and brought forward.

We watched from a distance as each of our five horses was run into the squeeze and a little trap-door was opened by the head so that the BLM staff could halter them. The horses were used to the padded crush, having been in it many times during their time in captivity for vet work, branding and hoof care. The squeeze could be tilted on its side, and many small doors allowed access to any part of the horse with minimal damage to both horse and handler.

The haltered Mustangs were then directed into the crush, and Amanda's boldly took the lead, leaping up the small step into the trailer with the other four following close behind. The door was quickly closed and latched, and we were on the road. Arriving at Matt and Stacie's, we unloaded and settled the horses with food and water; they were all stressed, so we headed inside to eat and left them to relax for a few hours. We weren't in a hurry to begin working with them, wanting them to be in a better frame of mind before training began. Meanwhile, we pored over their paperwork and began coming up with names. All five of our horses were from different herd management areas in Oregon. My mare was a six-year-old from Jackies Butte and had been mustered four years earlier; Amanda's was a five-year-old from Sand Springs, Vicki's and Alexa's were both six-year-olds, from Murderers Creek and Coyote Lake, respectively, and Kirsty's was a five-year-old from Three Fingers. We came up with names based on where they had been mustered from and decided to try out Jackie, Spring, Red Rum (murder backwards), Coyote and Digit (a number and also a finger) for the next few days to see if they suited each horse's personality.

In the late afternoon we headed back outside to see the property full of action. One of the trainers was working with their Mustang in the indoor arena and it was already lathered in sweat. The confused horse was being worked in the round pen until it learnt to maintain rhythm and turn towards the inside when it was asked to change direction on a circle; it was a little cut-up from crashing into the rails. We left them to continue their session while we went in search of long grass to pick. Our first goal was to get our horses used to our presence and hopefully eat grass from our hands. We didn't want to scare them or establish ourselves as a threat, and were planning to spend a few hours essentially doing nothing with them.

The Mustangs were significantly quieter than the wild Kaimanawas we were used to dealing with, and we were able to stand in the corner of their yards (with the gates unlatched in case we needed to make a quick escape), talking quietly. My mare, Jackie, was the most stressed, but even she just watched me warily; she would only spin and pin herself against the rails as far from me as possible if I moved, so I was careful to keep my body language quiet. The Kaimanawas would have been trying to crawl over the rails to escape if we'd tried to get this close so soon after they had arrived — it was a huge help having the horses already accustomed to fences. After a couple of hours of me standing still, doing nothing, Jackie turned and faced me, and stretched out her neck to sniff the grass in my outstretched hand before leaping back again. Happy with her progress, I left the grass in the yard for her to eat, quietly opened the gate and went to see how the others were doing.

In the next yard over, Alexa was working with her mare, Coyote. Unlike Jackie, who had at least stood facing me, Coyote had her head in the corner hiding — her first instinct was to use her hind legs to protect herself from a perceived threat. It took a lot of time and careful reading of the horse's body language before the defensive mare finally turned and faced Alexa, who was quick to reward her by leaving the yard and giving her time to think things over.

Further along, Vicki, Amanda and Kirsty were working patiently with their horses. Over the two hours, the horses had progressed from standing in a corner of their yards to stepping forward. My sisters both had lead ropes on their Mustangs and had touched their heads for the first time, and Kirsty was standing beside Digit's shoulder and stroking her matted coat, although Digit wouldn't let her touch her head and kept it lowered, trying to ignore Kirsty.

Deciding that the horses had made enough progress for now, we headed back to the indoor arena to watch one of the other Mustangs being worked in the round pen. Like the first horse we'd watched, this Mustang had learnt to maintain rhythm and turn in on the circle; we watched while the trainer went on to lasso it and then flick the rope all over it. Initially the horse panicked, running into the rails, but eventually she stood still, her sides heaving, while she was touched all over her body; first with a rope and then a human hand, before the trainer jumped up and lay over her back to get her accustomed to bearing the weight of a rider.

The method was certainly different from our own, with much faster results. We were interested to watch the other trainers work to see if we could pick up small things that would improve our own way of training, but more importantly we were interested in seeing how their horses mentally coped with the pressure they were under. Sometimes being exposed to too much, too fast, can make a horse shut down. We have developed methods specifically designed to ensure that the horses are dictating the time-frame of their training so that they develop as happy horses that want to work with us through mutual trust and respect. It was interesting watching horses work that didn't have the option to progress at their own pace.

Already we were seeing differences between the horses. On one side of the barn, our horses stood dozing. If someone walked past them they would watch intently, but they were generally relaxed and we could safely enter their yards to muck out around them and change their food and water. On the other side of the barn, the two Mustangs that had already been worked were standing worried and on edge; dry sweat making their coats appear starry. Three other Mustangs who were yet to be worked were also worked-up, reacting to the tension from the others. It wasn't that they'd been ill-treated — by most standards the training methods were considered gentle in the Wild West, where 'rough and ready' training practices were once commonplace. Some of the techniques the other trainers were using weren't that different to what we did, but the order they did them in was vastly different — their Mustangs had been required to cope with things in the first few hours of handling that we would only try days or weeks later, once the horses trusted us completely and understood that there was no reason to fear humans.

Watching the other horses being worked brought to mind the conversation from earlier about the Mustangs having natural predators and how this makes them more reactive. While the point had merit, we were left thinking that if you don't act like a predator then the horse won't react like prey — surely, if you don't give the horses a justifiable reason to either take flight or fight, most of the battles between horses and humans can be avoided.

By the end of the first day, having sat quietly with our Mustangs again in the evening, we were exhausted but pleased with how they were accepting us. Alexa and I were by far the most patient and had been assigned the horses that needed the most time; Kirsty, the shortest of the five of us, was paired up with the smallest mare. Amanda had the cheekiest and Vicki had an athletic type that tried hard to please — so we were all very well matched with our horses in terms of size and

Our Mustangs loading onto
the trailer at the BLM yards.

personality. As we headed inside for dinner we couldn't help but smile; although our horses were well behind some of the others, we were more than satisfied with our day's work. While our Mustangs were obviously going to be a challenge, especially Jackie and Coyote, that's the norm with wild horses and we weren't worried.

WE SET OUR ALARMS FOR 6 A.M. the next morning — there was a lot to get done before we set off to Wyoming in two days' time, and an early start meant that we could work the horses twice with plenty of time for them to rest in between. Considering the limited facilities and how wild the Mustangs were, it was incredibly ambitious of us to expect to have all five horses handled enough to lead and load onto a trailer in just a couple of days.

Freezing winds greeted us as we stepped outside, and dark clouds were blocking the early morning sun. A storm was rapidly approaching, but as time was short we bundled up in jackets and made a bee-line for the barn to muck out and get the Mustangs reacquainted with us. Even though the horses had made good progress yesterday, we started from scratch — assuming that they had remembered nothing — to make sure we didn't rush them or ask for more than they were ready for. Gradually over the next half-hour, we got them used to our presence again, and repeated their previous lessons before asking them to learn something new.

By the end of the day we were able to touch all five horses, although some were significantly more advanced than others. Red, Digit and Spring were confident about being touched on the head, neck and shoulders, while Alexa and I were struggling: both of our mares were cautious and hesitant to be approached or touched. We started thinking outside the box. At home, with the wild Kaimanawas, we occasionally teach them to lead before the horses are confident about being touched, but here — with no ropes on the horses and no facilities to aid the process — we had to improvise. From a short distance away I looped a lungeing whip through the halter, then attached a rope to the end before threading it back through, tying it and pulling the loop tight. With my mare now on a rope, I opened the gate into the aisle and worked with her quietly in a less confining area. Jackie was far more engaged out of her yard, and every time I lifted my hand she stretched her head forward to interact with me instead of trying to keep as much distance between us as possible. Soon we had our first touch on the head, and thrilled with her improved attitude I set her loose.

Seeing how much progress Jackie had made, Alexa asked me to show her how I'd got the rope on, and soon Coyote was also caught. Because Coyote had a tendency to be defensive, Alexa stayed on the other side of the fence rather than working in the yard beside her, but soon she was touching Coyote on the head and neck without the mare trying to hide. Generally pleased with our horses, we then all headed inside for the night.

The next day we rose early again; we were making the most of the time available, but at the same time carefully balancing this against the horses' welfare to ensure that they weren't having too much contact time. If needed, we could delay our departure, although it would mean Vicki and Amanda missing out on Las Vegas, where the World Cup Show Jumping and Dressage Finals happened to be taking place. We'd only allowed four days to prepare the horses for travelling, and two days to drive to Wyoming and get the Mustangs settled, before they would have to fly out to Vegas. Vicki and Amanda, who compete professionally to World Cup level, would watch and learn from some of the world's best riders, at the highest level of competition. It was poor timing, considering that they had wild horses to work, but a few days off after an intensive week would be good for the horses, and it was too good an opportunity for Vicki and Amanda to miss.

On their third handling session, and after spending less than two hours of contact time with Red, Vicki had her responding to gentle pressure on the rope, and so opened the gate to lead her down the aisle to an outdoor pen so she could be worked in a larger space. Red was willing but cautious as she followed Vicki past the other horses, pausing in confusion when she got worried. Step by step they made progress, but at the gate she froze, uncertain. Since Red was still getting used to pressure on a rope, and was confused by what was being asked of her,

Top
Amanda standing quietly in the entrance of Spring's yard to get the mare accustomed to humans.

Bottom
Jackie initiating human contact for the first time, two days out of the BLM yards.

Vicki asked one of us to step behind her. This works quite well with the Kaimanawas when they freeze, encouraging them to take hesitant steps forward, but Red's reaction was totally different — overly reactive, she rushed through the open gateway. Unable to hold Red because of her still healing shoulder, Vicki dropped the rope and stepped aside until the mare settled. Once she was calm, Vicki stepped forward to retrieve the rope and continued the session.

It was only the first of many times that we would see how a truly wild horse's reactions differ from a BLM Mustang's. While in some ways the Mustangs were significantly easier, we were quickly discovering that in other areas they were more difficult. One of the most obvious differences showed up when leading the horses down narrow raceways; we assumed this was because the Mustangs were used to being sorted and drafted down races in the BLM yards, they would panic and rush forward if they saw people behind them.

Vicki soon had Red leading and standing to be brushed on both sides of her body. Feeling that the mare was ready for a new challenge she led her back down the aisle, careful to keep her relaxed, and into the Western arena. Again Red was significantly more worried in the narrow race, but once she was through the gate and in an open area again she settled quickly. While Vicki played with Red in the arena, Kirsty made the most of the larger pen to work with Digit in the open and get her leading. The little black mare was the most inquisitive of the five and the first to be touched, and would now stand with her head resting on Kirsty's shoulder while Kirsty brushed her. It was obvious that Digit was starting to trust Kirsty and was enjoying human attention.

Even Amanda was starting to win her mare over, but she had a different problem. Unlike the other Mustangs, which showed some caution, Spring wasn't scared of Amanda at all. While initially this made her handling quite easy, it soon proved to be worrying — once out of the comfort of the small yard, Spring found everything scary and used Amanda like a security blanket, leaping on top of her every time something startled or distracted her. The first few times was daunting for Amanda — after working with Hoff, a very challenging Kaimanawa stallion in New Zealand whose first instinct was to attack, she was uncomfortable and intimidated having a wild horse so up close and personal. However, she soon came to realise that, unlike Hoff, Spring was neither aggressive nor fearful of people. She was therefore less likely to try to flee or fight — in many ways, she was more like a pushy and unhandled young horse you might expect to get off a stud, than a once-wild horse. Because of this, Amanda worked differently with her than she would with any other wild horse: the focus was more on setting boundaries, through gentle but firm means, than on trying to build a friendship. Slowly but surely, Spring came to understand that she needed to respect Amanda's personal space, and Amanda felt much safer handling her when the 500-kilogram mare wasn't climbing all over her.

Unlike Spring, both Jackie and Coyote were genuinely scared of people, although both reacted in different ways. Slowly we made progress, however, and soon they were standing to be touched on the neck. Giving them a break, we headed to town to watch a movie and collect the trailer, which was now road-legal.

WE RETURNED TO WORK THE HORSES LATER that afternoon, and within minutes Digit and Red were caught up on everything they had learnt so far. Deciding that Digit was ready for the Western arena, Kirsty led her out, following closely behind Red, but when Digit neared the gate she reared and spun, bolting back to the safety of her yard. Coaxing her forward again, they made it down the aisle a second time, before Digit panicked again and bolted back. The third time, Amanda, Alexa and I stood at the corner; when Digit spun, she paused when she saw a human barrier blocking her path, giving Kirsty a chance to settle her down and get her relaxed before asking her forward through the gate again. This time Digit followed, and once she was in the large arena she relaxed. Soon both Digit and Red were working over obstacles: standing on boxes, walking across bridges and weaving between cones. Both horses were very smart and willing to try new things even when they were unsure; it was remarkable to see how far they had come in less than three days.

To reward the horses, Vicki and Kirsty led them out to the pasture to graze; it was their first time out of a yard since they had been mustered from the wild. In the next field they let the Mustangs splash in a shallow stream, and since the horses were enjoying themselves they waited patiently on the bank to let them have their fun. For almost half an hour the horses splashed, rolled in the stream and nibbled on the grass at the water's edge, and finally as the sun set they were led, dripping wet, back to their yards. It was wonderful to see the horses get so much pleasure from such a small adventure, and we were keen to get them all out and about to show them more of the world — it was hard to comprehend just how boring they must have found the past few years of their lives in the BLM yards.

Meanwhile, Amanda, Alexa and I had made good progress familiarising our horses to human touch. All three also understood the basics of leading, and Amanda soon had Spring out on the Western arena navigating the obstacles, although she was still more easily distracted and slightly ADHD when asked to do new things.

Jackie had a highly developed flight mode, more so than the others. If she was startled by something, she would leap away and flee, as fast and as far as possible in the opposite direction. Even leading her in a small yard was challenging in the first few days. The first time she got away from me she panicked about the dragging lead rope, galloping around in circles until she realised it wasn't hurting her. When she finally stood still, I had to start from the basics again, trying to convince her that she had no reason to worry. Finally, I got her to the point where she would follow me on a loose lead, and we inched our way down the aisle back to her yard to give her a rest before we tackled the larger arena.

Alexa set to work in the round pen with Coyote, who was quickly developing a reputation for being the most difficult of the five. Over the past three years we had trained more than 30 wild horses, but Coyote's reactions were unlike anything we had encountered from a previously untouched horse; she lacked the instinctive responses we'd come to associate with wild horses. Although the BLM had assured us that none of the horses in the Extreme Mustang Makeover had been handled

Top
After just three days, Digit and Red could be trusted to lead in the pasture and they loved splashing and rolling in the creek.

Bottom
In contrast, by the evening of our third day, Jackie and Coyote were highly sensitive and reactive, at times barely able to be led.

previously, we still wondered whether perhaps she'd actually been re-homed and then returned to the BLM yards. With over 50,000 wild horses in their yards, it was certainly plausible that paperwork could get confused. The wild BLM Mustangs are available for adoption for US$150, but if returned they can then be purchased for just US$25. If they are returned a second time, their price drops to a mere US$10. If the third home doesn't work out, they become known as 'three-strike' horses — deemed unsuitable for re-homing — and are branded with a large number on their rumps before being sent to join the older horses in the long-term holding facilities, where they generally live out their lives.

Coyote reminded us of an abused horse more than a wild horse. It was unsettling seeing her react to so many situations in ways we had only encountered in horses that had previously been mistreated. Although she now stood to be approached and touched, when Alexa took her hands off or turned to leave, Coyote would pin her ears back and snake her head at her. Even more worrying, when she was let loose in the round pen, she would open her mouth like a bucking bronco and self-lunge around Alexa without being asked. She would maintain a rhythm while stamping her forelegs angrily on the ground, broncoing and striking out as she cantered around and around the outside, but as soon as Alexa stepped back, the mare would stop and turn to the inside, standing to wait for directions — a learnt behaviour, if ever we'd seen one; something wild horses don't instinctively do.

With only a day left before the horses needed to be taught to load, and darkness approaching, Alexa led Coyote out to the Western arena to get her accustomed to the obstacles. I caught Jackie and decided to join them. Having the worst two horses on the arena at the same time proved to be a terrible idea. Jackie panicked and bolted, galloping blindly with me skating along behind, half being dragged and half running, to keep up. Determined not to let go, I hung on; it was crucial that the mare learnt she couldn't just leave. Jackie's galloping set Coyote off, and there was chaos as Coyote got free and bolted.

Finally, Jackie turned to face me, rearing up and striking the air in fury; I stood panting as the defiant mare came to earth and stood watching me. Behind us, Alexa had caught Coyote; and slowly we began working with them again. Within 10 minutes, Alexa had her mare on the smaller box, but I didn't even bother trying. It was hard enough getting Jackie anywhere near the obstacles scattered around the arena and I could barely touch her, although she had been making good progress in the comfort of her yard. Exhausted, and running out of daylight, we put the horses away for the night and headed inside. We had just one more day to get our Mustangs loading on the trailer, and we were unsure just how many of them would be ready for *that* milestone.

The last 15 minutes of the road
to our Wyoming host ranch was
slick with mud and snow, and in
one of the most remote locations
we had ever encountered.

CHAPTER 3

Road trip from hell

The next morning, two of the other five trainers based at the property were ready to load and leave. Both horses had made quick progress — they had been backed, had a surcingle (a training strap that fastens around the horse's middle) and a saddle blanket on, were leading, picking up all four feet, lungeing on both reins and would lie down with ropes on. Watching the trainers work during the day, and often well into the night, had been an insightful experience and if anything had made us appreciate our own approach with the wild ones.

Many times the other trainers had offered to help us speed up the process as they walked past, joking that we were going to love our horses into submission. Each time we'd smiled and said we were happy with how the horses were coming along — and we truly were. If you give horses enough time and love in those first few weeks, they become partners and equals, which sets them up for the rest of their domesticated lives.

Since the other Mustangs were being loaded in the round pen, right outside our horses' stalls, Alexa and I led Jackie and Coyote out onto the Western arena; we didn't want them unsettled by watching the other horses being loaded. Alexa soon had Coyote on a box and they quickly worked through all the obstacles; the chestnut mare was relaxed and curious as she explored and conquered everything asked of her. For 30 minutes, Jackie inched closer to the first box — just 10 centimetres above the ground — eventually raising one foreleg and pawing it before rushing backwards in fright. After that she wouldn't approach anything, and at times she would be so unsettled she would refuse even to lead.

We were keeping one eye on the two Mustangs that were still trying to load; eventually, they had to back the trailer up to the aisle and chase them onto it. This didn't bode well for Jackie, who in comparison was significantly less handled. I was unsure whether I should even attempt to load her, or just run her up the race from the beginning to avoid the potential stress.

Soon afterwards, Vicki, Amanda and Kirsty returned from another adventure with the Mustangs down at the stream and we left the horses to eat while we headed inside to pack our bags and prepare ourselves for travel. Just before dusk, we backed the trailer up to the yards for a practice loading — we were leaving at sunrise, and with such a long drive ahead of us it was important that we weren't delayed getting the horses to load the following morning. Our trailer had no ramp and the step up was quite high, so we positioned one of the boxes as a step to make it easier for the horses. Red was the first to go, and in under two minutes she bravely stepped into the trailer, turned quietly and unloaded with minimal hesitation. Spring, Digit and Coyote went next, in turn, and they too loaded in just a couple of minutes without stressing.

Since the others had been so easy, I decided to attempt loading with Jackie. It would be far less stressful on her if she could be led on rather than being herded, and far safer if we had to unload along the way. My expectations were very low, however. I got everyone to back away from the trailer so that Jackie wouldn't be worried about people behind or to the side of her. Stepping up into the trailer I allowed Jackie to lower her head and look at the box, something she hadn't relaxed enough to do in the arena. Stepping hesitantly forward, she lowered her head — and then to my surprise she lifted a foreleg and walked straight in beside me and stood there, relaxed, while I patted her. It had taken less than a minute, and I was the one in shock.

Relieved, I unloaded Jackie, gave her a handful of fresh grass as a reward and led her back to her yard for the night. We could only hope that the horses would load this well in the morning!

WE WOKE BEFORE SUNRISE THE NEXT DAY to stormy weather and a bitter chill to the wind. The forecast was for snow in the mountains, and we hoped it would hold off long enough for us to get to Wyoming. The Mustangs did load without hesitation, and within minutes we had the ramp door closed and were on the road. Vicki carefully navigated the icy roads while the rest of us took turns sleeping. It started snowing two hours into our journey and, with equal amounts of excitement and trepidation, we watched the snowflakes land on the windows and the landscape gradually turn white.

About an hour later I was startled from sleep by the hoot of a horn, and quickly sat upright to glance out the window. A truck driver was waving us over to the side of the road and yelling something at us; worried, we stopped the truck on the interstate. Alexa and I piled out to see what was wrong, and as we circled the trailer were shocked when we saw the back door. It had two parts: it could either be opened fully like a door, which is what we'd done for loading, or half could open as a stock entrance. The narrower section hadn't been latched properly, and had fallen open with Digit's hindquarters clearly visible. We were fortunate we'd been travelling at a constant speed on straight roads — if Digit had needed to brace while we were going around a corner or accelerating, she could have fallen out and been severely injured, if not killed. After securing the door, we headed back to the truck and told Vicki what had happened. Paranoid, she made us go back and double-check before, chilled to the bone, we were allowed to settle back in our seats and layer on more clothing.

I drifted off to sleep again, but Vicki soon awakened me. The truck was losing power — she couldn't get it going faster than 50 miles (70 kilometres) per hour on the open, flat road. Concerned, we rang the dealers we'd bought it from and, following their advice, learnt how to pump fuel. Soon the truck was back on the road at full speed, and we relaxed. This only lasted half an hour, though, and soon we were pumping fuel every few miles to keep it going. It was a worrying time — caught in a snowstorm, on the interstate, with five barely handled Mustangs, a truck now doing only 25 miles (40 kilometres) per hour at full speed, and the closest town still miles away.

Finally, we crawled into Twin Falls after five hours of driving; it should have taken no more than three on a good day. Our first stop was the mechanic, who refused to look at the truck with the trailer attached. With no one else available until late afternoon, we drove off at a snail's pace to find a yard to put the horses in. The Livestock Commission's auction yards proved promising; when we explained our dilemma they agreed to give us the use of a yard while we got the truck repaired and back on the road.

We unloaded the horses separately to make them more manageable.

The yard was at the end of a long, narrow race — the Mustangs' tendency to flee down raceways had never been more evident, and it took every ounce of strength to hold them. With the first three Mustangs out of sight, Alexa and I unloaded our horses and set off after them. One of the cowboys shut the gate behind us and Jackie leapt forward, but with a firm grip on the rope I was able to stop her from bolting. With every step the horses grew more agitated, however, and when Jackie saw another person around the corner she lost it completely, bolting forward to gallop down the race and wrenching the rope from my hands. Not wanting to be left alone, Coyote bolted after her. Up ahead, the other three hadn't yet made it to the yard and, as Jackie and Coyote galloped down the race, the other horses panicked. We watched in horror as Kirsty was knocked to the ground and caught up underneath the stampeding horses as they leapt through the gateway and into their allocated yard. By the time we reached Kirsty, though, she was already standing and dusting the dirt from her clothes; although battered and bruised, she managed a small smile and followed us to the horses. It was the first time the Mustangs had been yarded together and, unsure how easy they would be to catch, we unclipped the ropes from the easiest three only, leaving Jackie and Coyote dragging theirs.

Once they'd been fed hay, we unhooked the trailer and returned to the mechanic, hoping that the problem would only be minor. A blocked filter was soon replaced and they took it for a test drive with no issues; we were fairly sceptical, though, since they had only driven a short distance without pulling a heavy load. We were advised to stay in the area, since it was already late afternoon and there was a possibility of the fuel injectors having to be replaced. This would cost between US$5000 and $9000 and would take at least a week; something we had neither the time nor the money for.

Concerned about the horses, we ignored the advice and decided to load up and keep driving, hoping that the mechanics had fixed the truck. The stockyards were next to the railway tracks, and with snow everywhere, night approaching and the fences too low for comfort, we weren't confident that the horses were safe there for the night. The ranch in Wyoming was less than six hours away, and if we left now and had no issues we could arrive before midnight.

Wanting to avoid the horses panicking again, we let Vicki and Kirsty go ahead down the race. Once Digit and Red were safely in the smaller yard at the far end, we opened the gate and let the other three follow, rather than trying to lead them. As we walked after them we couldn't help overhearing the cowhands behind us comment that we were the finest-looking heifers they'd had in those yards. Laughing quietly, we quickly caught up to the horses, who had cantered well ahead, and set to work catching them. Jackie repeatedly dodged me, and Amanda and Alexa weren't having much luck either, so Vicki took over, catching each of them and handing us their ropes.

Back on the interstate, with the truck running at full speed, it was a huge relief to have had such a quick and cheap solution to the issue. To our dismay, however, an hour and a half later the truck quit again, refusing to go above 25 miles per hour. With evening setting in, there was a very real possibility that we would be stranded in the worsening snowstorm at the side of the road.

Before long, a sign appeared — the town of Blackfoot was 40 miles away, and although it took us two hours to get there we finally arrived. Not knowing who might have suitable yards, we pulled over and Alexa jumped out to ask a guy on the side of the road for directions. Kirsty was freaking out, worried about how safe it was in this quiet ghost town, and regretting that she'd never taken self-defence classes. When Alexa leapt back in and told Vicki to follow the guy although she had no idea where he was taking us, had barely understood half of what he'd said and hoped he wasn't a serial killer, it was hardly reassuring. Kirsty mumbled something about our lack of firearms.

The stockyards duly appeared, and we waved cheerily at the guy as he turned and drove off, his car soon out of sight in the swirling snow. We quickly discovered that most of the yards were padlocked, but eventually found three that were accessible, and backed the trailer up to the race to unload. Jackie, Coyote and Spring went into one yard each, with Digit and Red left in the race together — at this point anything was better than nothing, and with snow settling on the horses and clinging to our clothes we headed off in search of a place to spend the night.

Exhausted, we stopped at a hotel and were disheartened to find it fully booked. As were the next three places. There were moments when we actually contemplated sleeping in the truck, we were so tired. Nearing midnight, however, we found a poorly signposted road which led us to the centre of town and finally found a hotel with one spare room; pushing the two queen beds together, we crammed the five of us on and fell into a deep sleep.

WE WOKE TO HEAVY SNOW BUT CLEAR BLUE SKIES, and feeling relieved we headed off to check the horses. The owners of the stockyards were already on-site, and when we explained the situation they were happy for the horses to stay in the yards until help arrived.

The night before, we'd called the dealers we'd purchased the truck from, and they had agreed to give us a full refund, send a driver to collect us and drive us the remaining five hours to the ranch, before returning and towing the broken truck back to their dealership. It was an incredibly generous offer, as we hadn't paid for a warranty and they really had no obligation at this point to help us. After such a stressful day, it was a huge relief to have bought a vehicle off people who were actually interested in their customers and were willing to go the extra mile — especially for five young foreign females who were turning out to be quite the liability!

Although it was still bitterly cold, we decided to make the most of the next few hours and handle the horses. If we actually made it to Wyoming tonight, the truck driver would also drop Vicki and Amanda off at the airport, and their two Mustangs wouldn't be worked for the next five days until they returned. Initially I'd been disappointed to miss out on the World Cup Finals, but now, with my mare taking so much time to win over, I was relieved to have the extra time to work with her.

Red, Spring and Digit, who were all able to be caught easily, were inquisitive and curious when approached, and the girls began handling them. Alexa and I opened the gates into our mares' yards and quietly began talking to them as we drew closer. As the yards were larger and our mares were so unsettled from being constantly on the move, we'd left lead ropes on them again overnight. Inching our way closer to them, we noticed something strange about the ropes — they weren't dragging like normal and instead were tangled around the horses' necks and through their halters. It wasn't until we had our hands on the horses that we discovered the ropes had actually been tied this way. It was astounding: we'd left the horses after dark and arrived the next day by 7 a.m., leaving very little time for someone to hassle the Mustangs, as they clearly had. It was just our luck that they'd chosen to harass the two most sensitive and worried of our horses. To my surprise, however, Jackie was actually easier to handle than normal after the encounter; but Alexa was struggling with Coyote. It took a lot of reassurance and softly spoken words to settle her enough to get the rope untied. We joked that a Native American horse-whisperer must have worked with Jackie overnight — and his apprentice must have messed around with Coyote.

The snow had begun to fall again, so we headed off for an early lunch to make sure we were back in time to meet the driver. He arrived in the early afternoon and we hitched up the trailer, loaded the horses and hit the road again. Hour after hour we watched as the landscape changed from desolate plains to snowy mountain passes scattered with iced-over lakes. Wyoming was beautiful in all her winter glory, and the impressive Grand Teton ranges were a breathtaking sight as we drew closer to our final destination. As the driver carefully navigated the final 15 minutes of gravel roads, we watched as wild elk and mule deer frolicked in the snow; it felt like we were in a movie — surely we'd seen no other place on earth this wild or remote.

Two days after we'd left Idaho, we arrived at the ranch — only to find a huge warning sign directing us to detour through the neighbour's property, due to the driveway being too icy to navigate safely. The neighbours' driveway wasn't much better, and our driver struggled to keep the truck on the steep and slippery dirt track as we dropped down into the valley floor below. We had finally arrived at our destination.

Top
Our Mustangs yarded overnight during a snowstorm in Blackfoot, Idaho.

Bottom
The drive from Idaho to Wyoming was a total whiteout, unlike anything we had ever seen.

CHAPTER 4

The wild Wild West

The corrals at our host ranch in Wyoming looked like something out of a Wild West movie.

Top
The little log cabin we lived in during our time in Wyoming.

Bottom
The landscape was desolate yet beautiful; we could hike for hours without seeing another living soul.

The next 30 minutes were spent unloading the horses and sorting them into yards. To our absolute shock, the dude ranch, although set up for 80 horses, had minimal facilities. We thought we'd asked all the right questions, but quickly discovered that the rustic railed fencing was 35 years old and not really sturdy enough to hold wild horses. Even worse, there was only one small round yard, a covered pen, a rock-hard arena, a large feeding pad, and three small paddocks with fencing too low to contain the Mustangs. The rest of the property was a 100-acre paddock, with the boundary fences on the ground; the rails had rotted and broken after the heavy winter snowstorms and there was nothing to stop our horses escaping. To our further dismay, we discovered that the ranch backed onto millions of acres of National Park. On one side was a wildlife reservation and on the other the Eastern Shoshone Indian Reservation, which backed onto the Shoshone National Forest that in turn bordered Yellowstone National Park — which stretched right up into Montana. If our horses got loose, we would be in serious trouble. There was nothing ideal about the situation, but we would just have to make the most of it.

Overwhelmed, but with few options, we let all the horses loose in the covered pen together; in this type of weather they needed shelter. Because there were pillars holding up the shelter and so many horses in together, it wasn't safe to leave the ropes on Coyote or Jackie; we unclipped them, hoping that we would be able to catch them in the morning.

Back at the trailer, Vicki and Amanda were frantically sorting through their suitcases, grabbing what they would need for Vegas. Our truck driver was dropping them off in Jackson for the night, and they would get a taxi to the airport first thing in the morning. As they left, Vicki set us an impossible task — find a truck in time to collect them in five days' time. It was safe to say that Alexa, Kirsty and I had a moment of mild panic at the daunting week ahead of us.

With darkness now setting in, the owners of the ranch showed us our new home for the next three months: a small, rustic log cabin. Downstairs it had an open-plan kitchen and living area with a log fire-place and a small bedroom, and upstairs four of us would bunk in the loft. Exhausted, we fell into bed and hoped that tomorrow would prove to be less stressful than the past two days.

We woke early, dressed in multiple layers and made our way through the snow to check the horses. It was a good five minutes' walk to the yards, and by the time we got there our feet and hands were frozen. We had thought we were going to be in America for the summer, and had not anticipated being caught in a spring snowstorm. The horses were all relaxed and watchful as we approached. As they stepped through the snow towards us, it felt like we'd gone back in time — the wild Mustangs, rustic fencing, and snow contrasting against the red cliffs above was like a scene out of a Western movie of a bygone era. Since it was too cold to work with the horses, we tossed hay under the shelter and had breakfast with the ranch owners before returning to the cabin to finish sleeping.

OUR CABIN HAD NO INTERNET, NO PHONE, no television, no oven and no washing machine, and we had very little food left. Even worse, we had no way to drive to the closest town, which was 30 minutes away and had a population of 991, to shop for food or look for a new truck. We couldn't drive the owners' vehicle without being added to their insurance (which would have taken two weeks to arrange), so had to wait until they were going to town to catch a lift. To fill up time, we spent the afternoon playing with the Mustangs once the snow had melted away. One by one we caught them, starting with the easiest, until only Jackie remained. She, too, was soon caught, and we tied up Spring and Red while we worked with our own horses.

It was important that Vicki and Amanda's two Mustangs stretched their legs while they were away, so they had asked us to take them for walks, allowing the horses to get out of the yards and nibble on whatever vegetation they could find in this barren landscape. Worried about the possibility of the horses getting loose, however, we only worked them in the confines of the yards for the first couple of days. During this time we got our three used to being led around the yard, then accustomed to a saddle blanket. Kirsty even had Digit wearing a surcingle and trotting on the lunge on the first day.

Top
Coyote, with Alexa, grazing on the lake's edge.

Bottom
The view from our cabin; it wasn't uncommon to find moose, elk, mule deer or chipmunks outside.

On the third day we decided to venture further. Leading the Mustangs outside the yards was incredibly ambitious of us, considering the inadequate boundary fences and the endless expanse of open range, but we were careful to always keep one of the more settled horses, like Red or Digit, with the flightier ones to keep them relaxed. We could only hope that our Mustangs would return to their friends if they got away from us, or better yet that they wouldn't get loose at all. If something went wrong we faced the very real risk of losing our Mustangs in the wilderness and never seeing them again, but continuing to work the horses in a small area was boring for both us and them. We were desperate to get them out and show them the fun side of life.

The horses loved their first adventure, and especially enjoyed splashing in the pond and rolling in the freezing water. With nothing much else to do on the dude ranch during the off-season, and no other animals or people around, we sat with our horses for hours, letting them eat what tussock grass had survived the harsh winter. When we weren't working the Mustangs we explored, and on our first morning discovered a moose in the river, as well as countless gophers, mule deer and elk in the clearing outside our cabin.

In New Zealand, our lives are always on the go — we always have an adventure planned, dreams to conquer or competitions to attend — so it took us a while to appreciate the quieter side of life. Our enforced isolation and lack of technology encouraged us to draw, play cards, read books and go hiking. Each day we collected firewood, and we washed our clothes by hand and hung them to dry on baling twine we had set up between the trees. There were times when we were bewildered by our circumstances; this so wasn't what we thought we were getting ourselves into when we'd decided to base ourselves at a dude ranch in Wyoming.

The only thing that kept us sane was working the horses. Each day, we'd spend hours with them just so we didn't die from boredom. The Mustangs loved the extra attention and, although we spent longer with them than we would normally when training wild horses, it was a quiet and peaceful interaction. Training and working them lasted only 20 or 30 minutes, then the rest of the time we took them for adventures on the lead around the property or sat quietly listening to country music or reading while we held them to graze. The Mustangs came to enjoy their time with us, and each day were easier to catch and eager to get out and explore. After years of boredom and confinement in the BLM yards, we were offering them a better quality of life and they were starting to show both trust in and affection for us.

Nine days out of the BLM yards, and on just our third day at the dude ranch, we began asking more complicated things of our Mustangs. Rather than strolling around the property, we began going out of our way to find different things for the horses to walk over, on or under; as expected, the Mustangs found many of these new challenges scary and we had our first real battles. None more so than asking them to jump a small, shallow irrigation ditch that was no more than 30 centimetres wide and the same depth. Our Mustangs ranged between stubborn and outright defiant, rearing on the lead and refusing to step close to the ditch, let alone jump over it. With never-ending patience we waited for them to realise that what we were asking was neither impossible nor going to hurt them. Although some horses took five minutes and others half an hour, all five did eventually cross the ditch and land safely on the other side.

This taught the horses a valuable lesson about how to process the things we asked of them. When pressure was applied they learnt that if they fought, moved away from what was scaring them or tried to ignore us, the question would stay the same until they gave us the answer we were looking for. It was a dance of sorts: knowing exactly when to ask for more, when to wait, and when to reward the horses for trying, even if it was only a stretch of the neck, a licking of the lips, or a forward step. We never punished the horses or disciplined them for their antics. They were responding instinctively to a situation they didn't trust, and if we had punished them this would have only affirmed that there was indeed something either painful or worth fearing about the situation. Instead we waited patiently, rewarding positive behaviour, and gradually the horses settled and began trying for us. When each eventually built up the courage to jump the ditch, we rewarded them with a gentle pat and

TOP
Coyote lost her halter overnight, and although she was good to approach, it took some time before she would let Alexa re-halter her.

MIDDLE
Jackie and Red disagreeing about crossing a dry, shallow ditch.

BOTTOM
Kirsty lying across Digit's back for the first time, just eight days out of the BLM yards.

a handful of grass and moved on to easier things. It was important that the horses learnt to trust that we would only ask questions that wouldn't endanger them; overcoming these battles with a positive outcome was invaluable in developing a trusting and strong work ethic in our horses.

The following day they all jumped the ditch within seconds; so to further challenge the horses we asked them to walk over one of the narrow bridges that crossed the ditches. The lessons they had learnt the day before, jumping the ditch, had their effect — now, rather than trying to avoid what we were asking of them, they thought it through and tried. Although scared, they attempted everything, and with every forward step we spoke words of affirmation and released the pressure on the rope so that they could have time to relax and think. Surprisingly, it was Jackie and Coyote — the worst two from the day before — who confidently crossed the bridge within minutes; Digit, who was by far the most advanced, took the longest.

On day 11 we woke to fresh snow on the ground again, and went for a hike to enjoy the winter wonderland before heading down to catch the horses. Coyote, who was still one of the more difficult horses to catch, had lost her halter overnight and Alexa was thrilled when the mare approached her to be caught. Getting the halter on was a little more challenging, though, and a few times she took fright and retreated. Once she was successfully haltered, we headed out to practise crossing ditches and bridges again. From there, we led the horses onto the porches of the main lodge and asked them to stand with their front feet balanced on raised flower pots, jump over the logs around the camp fire, and then stand while we swung like children in the rope swing that hung from the tree.

With the horses so settled, we began backing them, getting them used to feeling our weight on their backs. Digit stood quietly while Kirsty jumped off the ground and lay across her back, and then started taking her first forward steps bearing the weight of a rider. Coyote and Jackie were, of course, more easily startled — my mare rushed backwards as soon as she felt my weight, and Alexa's horse would flatten her ears and get grumpy. For the next hour we worked the horses beside the campfire, balancing on the logs while we held them and gradually leant our weight over their backs until finally they stood still; although Coyote, in particular, wasn't happy about it and would need a lot more work. Pleased with how they had been working, we returned them to their yards and headed back to the cabin to handwash our clothes, collect more wood for the fire and tidy up the cabin before Vicki and Amanda arrived home later that afternoon.

UNFORTUNATELY WE HADN'T YET BEEN ABLE to buy a truck, although we'd managed to access the internet and had several lined up to see. The closest options were over an hour's drive away, and without a vehicle we hadn't been able to view anything. With no other option, Vicki and Amanda hired a rental car from the airport and drove the two hours back to the ranch.

As soon as they got back, they caught their Mustangs and headed out on an adventure. Vicki headed for the steep red cliffs that bordered the property, and as she climbed in altitude she discovered cactus plants. It was amazing that something you generally associate with the desert was found in an area that had been white with snow only that morning. Down below, Amanda was working with Spring, who didn't appreciate being separated from her friend and was throwing a tantrum, rearing and spinning in circles.

Nearby, off the beaten track, Alexa and Kirsty had discovered a barrel strung between four posts, and since we'd only just watched the movie *The Longest Ride* they knew exactly what it was for — practising bull riding. Leaping up onto the barrel, Alexa hung on tight while Kirsty and Amanda pulled the ropes to make it move violently to mimic the movements of an enraged bull. It obviously hadn't been used for a while, however — and the tugging on the ropes caused a rotten post to give way and Alexa crashed to the ground. The commotion made Spring leap sideways in fright; hoping to calm her, Amanda started up the hill following in Red's hoof-prints. From below they were just silhouettes, with red dust flying around them as the sun set behind the hill.

Next, Vicki and Amanda headed for the pond to let the horses splash

Top
Backing Jackie and Coyote for the first time around the
campfire 10 days after they were first touched.

Bottom
Amanda and Spring's first adventure on her return from Las Vegas.

in the water, and on the way they asked the horses to navigate the various obstacles and bridges they encountered. Although neither horse had been worked much over the past five days, luckily both had been so advanced beforehand that they weren't the worse for wear. Our three had benefited from the extra work, so all five horses were now pretty much on an even playing field. It would be interesting to see how they all progressed over the next week — we were sure most of them would be ready for their first rides.

The next day, we worked the horses only briefly before driving an hour south-east to a nearby town. As towns go it was fairly small, and after looking through car dealerships and at private listings we found no suitable trucks within our budget. We were cautious about buying anything in case it broke down again — once bitten, twice shy. Heading to the next town we looked at more options, but again found nothing. Depressed and getting desperate, we increased our budget by half, but still there was nothing. Unsure what to do, we rang the dealers we'd bought the original truck from, in Idaho, and asked if they had anything available in the increased price range. After having been so well looked after during the disaster of the first truck, we felt confident dealing with them again. They told us they would call back once they'd had a look through what they had available.

With Vicki and Amanda back with us, training began in earnest. The next day, Red and Spring had surcingles on for the first time, and Digit and Jackie moved on to saddles. Every time we handled the horses they increased significantly in confidence and we were able to ask more of them — with the exception of Coyote. She was progressing at a much slower pace and couldn't handle anything new; even getting hands on her each day was a challenge, and Alexa had to keep every movement slow and precise so that Coyote wouldn't react or leap away.

We still had far too much spare time in between working the horses, and after a week of playing cards and living the quiet life, this was starting to get old. Vicki and Amanda had no interest in sitting around all day either, so we started going out for longer hikes, leading the Mustangs. With only 100 acres available we soon ran out of places to explore, so the following day, at sunrise, we took the Mustangs into the Indian reservation that bordered the property.

We scrambled up sheer cliffs and weaved through cactus as we made our way up into the steep hills overlooking the ranch; the view from the top was spectacular. On our way back, we slid down a steep shale path, then ran along a dried-up river bed, our Mustangs trotting willingly behind on the lead. They were curious and brave as we navigated the uneven terrain, but a little unorthodox. These Mustangs might have been born wild, on rugged country, but since they had been captured they had been isolated with nowhere to roam and only a flat surface to stand on. It was obvious how much they were lacking in fitness and, although instinctively sure-footed and sensible in this kind of landscape, they were also finding their feet on less even ground. The further we travelled, the more confident their footfalls became, and by the time we returned to the ranch two hours later they were nimbly leaping off banks and side-passing jagged rocks; the Mustangs were starting to think like wild horses again and carefully considering where they placed each hoof to avoid injury.

That afternoon, the first of the ranch horses returned from winter grazing, complete with two overly friendly goats, an obese donkey and an overweight mule — both with early stages of laminitis. As we were still truckless, we asked for a lift to town and bought farrier tools to correctively trim the turned-up hooves of the donkey and the mule. We also took it upon ourselves to help manage their food, to try to lessen the chances of their health worsening. Next we set to work trimming the ranch horses' hooves, which were also in poor condition; some still sported shoes from six months earlier.

It was a great opportunity for Alexa, Kirsty and me to improve our skills. Vicki and Amanda, who were both experienced farriers, watched us work, offering suggestions and stepping in to do the worst of the corrective work. Now that we had the farrier tools, we also set to work teaching the Mustangs to pick up their hooves so that we could begin improving their hoof balance. In the BLM yards the horses are put in the squeeze once a year and tipped on their side to have their hooves

Top
Alexa and Coyote on top of the Red Cliffs in the Wind River valley.

Bottom
Vicki riding Red for the first time, the morning after she returned from Las Vegas.

ground down with electric tools to keep them short — it's a fast and effective method to prevent the hooves overgrowing and curling over. In the wild, a horse's hooves naturally wear down, as they travel such large distances, but in the yards, with limited space to move, the hooves continue to grow. Unfortunately, this method can create or exaggerate misshapen hooves, and three of our Mustangs were in need of some serious corrective trimming to straighten out their hoof balance. Unlike the ranch horses, which had overgrown hooves and plenty of hoof wall to work with, the Mustangs' hooves were so short that we only had millimetres to play with. It would take many months before the hoof wall would grow enough for us to be able to make significant changes to the shape of the hooves.

Late that afternoon, we returned to the yards and worked with the Mustangs again. Vicki and I sat astride our horses for the first time, a real milestone, and both horses were relaxed about the entire process. Kirsty was well advanced, confidently walking Digit around the yard, and Amanda lay across Spring for the first time as well as removing her BLM tag. Progress was definitely being made. Alexa, who was still struggling to get Coyote to tolerate her standing beside her shoulder, continued to work patiently, knowing it would pay off in the long run.

THE FOLLOWING WEEK FELL INTO A ROUTINE. We'd hike out in the morning, leading the horses to build up their fitness and give them an adventure, then in the afternoons we would work them in the arena; first backing, then riding, them. The horses loved their time out in the wilderness. Whenever we reached a sandy river bed they would drop to their knees and roll, and if we passed tussock grass they would stop to eat the dried stalks. Even though it was spring, the landscape showed no signs of life — very rarely did we see wildlife, and the trees and shrubs were barren and brown.

Every day something made us smile. The horses were loving life and their personalities were starting to shine through. Each time we achieved something new, like a first trot or picking up a hoof for the first time, it left us buzzing. Of course it wasn't *always* smooth sailing, and every now and again things didn't quite go to plan. The second day I sat on Jackie, I was laughing at a joke one of the others had made and Jackie took an unexpected step to the side. As it was her first time moving with a rider on, and I was distracted, I bailed — thinking she'd react and catch me off-guard. Instead of preventing a negative experience, however, I created one: my quick movement caused Jackie to leap forward and I lost my balance with one leg caught halfway over her back before falling awkwardly, my legs flipping over my head as I landed in a heap on the hard ground. Brushing myself off, I re-mounted and we stood quietly for a bit before I put her away and stiffly made my way back to the cabin. I was very annoyed with myself.

Another major, and avoidable, disaster was Digit getting loose. Kirsty had been out for a walk with Alexa, and they'd been letting the horses play in the swift-flowing river. Digit had stepped over her rope and got it tangled around her leg; rather than getting her boots wet while untangling the ropes, Kirsty had decided to wait and hope it would sort itself out. Instead, the mare headed deeper into the river, and with no leverage Kirsty couldn't turn her back and had to let her go. Digit disappeared out of sight; then we saw her 10 minutes later, galloping with her rope flying, under the cliffs bordering the Indian reservation and only a stone's throw away from the broken fence line. Digit neighed out in distress and Red replied; on hearing her, Digit turned and cantered back, eventually allowing Kirsty to catch her.

Sometimes things that went wrong weren't avoidable, but rather a process we had to patiently work through. Coyote represented one of these, constantly challenging us to re-evaluate and try new things. Although she'd come to accept Alexa touching her, she was still defensive if anyone else approached and wouldn't tolerate anything near her; nor did she like being told what to do. Wearing a saddle blanket — something the other Mustangs were quite accepting of — was a huge milestone for Coyote to reach; long before it got close to her, she would rear and strike out. Rather than punish the overly reactive mare, we patiently repeated the process despite only minuscule improvement each day, until finally she stood and coped with it.

At sunrise on day 16 we woke to a total white-out: a deep layer of snow covered the ground, and more was falling. The change in weather took us completely by surprise after days of warm weather and blue skies. Enthralled by the beauty of this frozen world, we dressed warmly and trudged through the deep snow in search of the corrals. Soon snow clung to our eyelashes, and our feet and hands were cold even through our riding boots and gloves. While the rest of the country was sensibly either sleeping or keeping warm in front of a fire, we fumbled with our Mustangs' halters. Once they were all caught we headed towards the hills, the horses' hooves crunching in the snow as we walked. Along the river we wandered, with snow continuing to fall as we crossed the bridge and headed into the trees. The trails were eerily quiet, and the Mustangs followed closely behind us, snatching hay from our hands as we walked.

By the time we made it to the sandy river bed the snow had stopped, and Vicki decided to give Red her second ride, again bareback in a halter. For 15 minutes she repeated the lessons from several days earlier, and soon she was sitting upright, one leg on either side of the mare, and asking her to step forward for the very first time. Step by step Red grew accustomed to her rider's weight, and, although initially unbalanced and unsure, she soon relaxed and followed Kirsty, who was riding Digit, down the river bed while Amanda, Alexa and I trailed behind leading our horses.

When they reached the river, Vicki waited behind so that Amanda could ride Spring across the river with Digit. Amanda came back halfway, but Kirsty and Digit crossed to the far side and went exploring along the river bank. When asked to turn back, Digit refused — she was more interested in exploring than returning to her friends. For the next 10 minutes she and Kirsty battled through their first argument; a daunting experience. So often with young or wild horses, everything is fun and games when they are enjoying themselves or going where they want, but eventually they have to learn to accept the directions of their riders and often it brings out the worst in them. Digit's tantrum was soon over, however, and she turned and crossed the river; Kirsty rewarded her with a pat. It was another lesson learnt for the little black mare, who was probably a week ahead of the rest of our horses.

While we'd been waiting for Kirsty, Vicki had been continuing to work with Red, teaching her to turn and halt when asked with the softest contact. It was the first time that Red had followed the direction and feel of her rider, as opposed to following Digit, and she was slowly gaining confidence. Since Jackie had now been sat on twice, I decided I'd try to ride her along the sandy river bed as well — it was far softer than the arena I'd fallen off onto the day before. I got her standing while I used the bank to lie over her back, and although she shifted forward the first few times, unsure about the rustling of my winter jacket, she soon relaxed and stood patiently while I sat upright. Applying gentle pressure with my legs, I got her to take our very first wobbly step, before halting and rewarding her. Confident that Jackie was relaxed and ready for more, we continued on, Kirsty taking the lead while Vicki and I followed. Five minutes later we turned off from the river bed and climbed up a big bank. At the top I dismounted to lead Jackie; the track narrowed ahead and I didn't want to weave between the shrubs and trees on a recently-backed Mustang.

Vicki decided to stay on Red, but soon lived to regret it. As they rounded a tight corner, Vicki's leg brushed up against a shrub, causing snow to fall. Red leapt forward in fright, causing more snow to fly; the startled mare dropped her head and spun on the narrow track to dart back the way she had come. The sudden movement caused Vicki to pitch off her shoulder. As Red leapt to safety she alarmed Jackie, who pulled the rope from my hands and followed the fleeing bay. A hundred metres away the two Mustangs stopped, watching us warily as we slowly approached and caught them before leading them home.

By the time we returned to the cabin, much of the snow had melted. Vicki re-mounted Red, who was still worried after losing her rider, and worked quietly with her to rebuild her trust. It took 20 minutes before she relaxed enough to be at the same stage she'd been before the fall. Meanwhile, Kirsty was making fine progress — since their battle on the river bank, Digit now understood about direction and leg. Soon they were powering through the last of the snow. The smile on Kirsty's face was contagious.

TOP
Hiking out in the snow
with the Mustangs to enjoy
the stunning landscape.

MIDDLE
Kirsty and Digit's first
trot, on our return from
hiking in the snow.

BOTTOM
Jackie and I out
in the snow.

Hiking with the Mustangs became a daily occurrence, both to avoid boredom and to build the horses' fitness.

CHAPTER 5

Problem children

Although we were satisfied with our Mustangs' progress, we were growing bored with the daily routine. Only having one horse each to work wasn't filling many hours of the day; unused to being idle, we weren't sure what else to do. Playing cards had got *really* old, we'd run out of books and there wasn't a centimetre of ground within hiking distance that we hadn't explored. Although we normally get on well, we weren't used to living on top of each other like this and were slowly getting on each other's nerves. There was no doubt that we needed something drastic to change — and fast — if we were going to survive for the next few months.

A few times we thought about going on a road trip through Montana, or riding through the nearby National Parks, but these kinds of adventure were weeks away — we needed to be able to reliably catch all of the horses in large paddocks and have them safe to ride in the hills before we ventured out into open country. There is nothing more daunting than the risk of taking wild horses out into wide open spaces and losing them. Committed to a certain amount of boredom in the short term, we continued working with the horses — the sooner they were working properly under saddle, the sooner we could start having adventures.

Now that the ranch horses were back and their hooves were trimmed, we decided to take some for a ride. Having quiet and dependable horses out alongside the Mustangs would be beneficial, so we thought we'd give them a trial run to make sure they would be good lead horses. Amanda took an older chestnut out bareback and the rest of us threw on Western saddles before mounting. Digit, who was yarded in the corrals beside the hitching rails, panicked when she saw us sitting on ranch horses and went galloping around the corral. Hoping she'd relax, we kept our horses steady — but instead she galloped for the gate, smashing into it and breaking the latch. The gate swung wide open and at a gallop Digit joined the 20 ranch horses in the feeding pad, warily watching us as she snorted and spun in circles. To make matters worse, it was the first time Digit had been loose with no halter. Kirsty quickly dismounted and rushed over to catch her, surprised when the mare trotted up to meet her and stood quietly to be haltered. Taking Digit to the arena, Kirsty let her loose with our other Mustangs so that the other horses would provide a buffer between her and us, and also some company.

After our ride, Kirsty headed over to catch Digit again; it was time for her first ride in a saddle. Although Kirsty was slightly cautious after Digit's earlier antics, she'd laid down good groundwork and was sure the mare was ready for the next step. They'd even had their first canter bareback out on the trails the day before, although the mare had left the path and leapt over a sage bush, causing Kirsty to lose balance and face-plant; she was hoping that the next canter, under saddle, would go a little better. Mounting carefully into the saddle, she made sure to sit quietly at first, to give the mare time to adjust to the new experience. Since Digit was obviously not worried, Kirsty urged her into a walk and then a trot, and Digit worked like a seasoned pro. After a little convincing from Vicki and me, Kirsty rode her out into the larger area where the ranch horses were kept, to try her first canter, and sure enough it was a success — Digit was one of the most willing wild horses we'd worked with, and we couldn't wait to get the rest of the Mustangs to the same stage.

BY DAY 22, ALEXA AND COYOTE WERE FINALLY ready for the next step, and Alexa sat on her for the first time. Coyote had been improving every day, and was now accepting Alexa in her personal space and allowing her to lie across her back while bearing her full weight. Alexa now worked with her in the smaller yard, bareback in a halter. Unlike many trainers, we didn't run our mares into the ground so that they were exhausted before the backing process begun. Nor did we begin the process before the horses were ready — we do not aim to 'bronc out' horses or break their spirit, instead making the backing process a natural progression of their handling. Over the next hour, Alexa jumped up and lay over Coyote's back, then stretched her legs over the mare's rump before eventually sitting up. Everything was going well, and Coyote stood, half asleep, while Alexa patted her and chatted with Amanda, who was watching from the rails. In the next corral, horses wandered over to drink from the water trough; when one lifted a hoof and caused the metal to clang, Coyote leapt in the air in fright — and Alexa, who

Top
Kirsty and Digit's first ride in a saddle and first canter on day 19.

Bottom
Jackie's first time saddled.

was holding the rope only loosely and not paying attention to her horse, went flying through the air.

Shaking her head in annoyance, Alexa dusted herself off and went to catch Coyote. She had worked with enough young horses in her time to know to keep a watch on her surroundings. So many falls happen not because the horse is uncomfortable having a rider, but because silly things startle them; Alexa knew she shouldn't have let herself become preoccupied. If she'd seen the ranch horses approaching, she could either have dismounted or had better control of the rope, allowing Coyote to have a positive first ride. Now, she had to start from scratch and make sure the mare didn't throw her off again. It had been an extreme reaction from Coyote, and Alexa would not take her for granted again; other horses might have just shied sideways, but Coyote's instinctive reaction had been to leap in the air and twist. Now that she'd lost her rider once, Coyote tried it again, and twice more in the next few minutes she tensed and leapt. Each time Alexa was prepared — rather than falling, she jumped off and stood beside the mare to reassure her before re-mounting and continuing. Eventually Coyote stood quietly with Alexa on her back, and she was rewarded with a gentle pat, led back to her yard and set loose with the other Mustangs. It hadn't been the best start to Coyote's ridden career, but they had finished on a good note and hopefully the next day would be better.

Later that afternoon we headed down to the river with Jackie, Digit and Spring. It was Amanda's first ride out of the yards, and not wanting two inexperienced horses to alarm each other I dismounted and held Jackie; she grazed while Digit and Spring went ahead. After riding along both river banks, they recrossed the river to join me. Amanda was unable to contain her smile — Spring was a gorgeous young mare with a great attitude to life. While we talked, Jackie tugged on the lead rope and I followed her to the river's edge, but instead of drinking she dropped to her knees and rolled in the freezing water. Laughing, I watched her wallow; when she finally stood up, dripping wet, I led her to the bank and jumped on. Following behind Kirsty, we crossed the river and I spent some time teaching Jackie to turn and halt; she was still quite reliant on following the other horses, and I had to be firm to get her to turn away and work independently.

Suddenly Jackie froze and turned her head towards the path leading to the corrals, and I looked up. Vicki was riding Red, saddled and stepping out nicely, down to join us; we recrossed the river to meet her. Wanting a lead, Vicki asked Kirsty to head back into the water to give Red confidence. Bravely the bay mare followed Digit into the fast-flowing water, but at the deepest point the swirling water caused her tail to tangle around her hocks and, unsettled, she spun around and headed for the safety of solid ground. The sudden movement combined with the tightening of the girth caused Red to panic; dropping her head, she leapt out of the water, lost her footing and fell. Vicki, unable to hold on as her shoulder was still sore from being dislocated five weeks earlier, went flying, hands-first. As the sodden horse and rider emerged from the churned-up water, it was obvious that Vicki had hurt herself; she was holding the reins gingerly, with her wrist held against her body to avoid jarring it. Luckily it wasn't serious — although it was sore because she'd broken that hand the previous year, after being careful with it for a few days she was fine.

Over the next couple of days the horses continued to advance in leap and bounds. Digit was now well established under saddle, was confidently cantering everywhere and continued to give confidence to the others. Jackie and Spring had their first trots bareback — not in a contained arena like you might expect, but in a large, open field, following behind Digit. Both horses were uncomplicated and strode out well — by now we'd had so many rides on the horses that they were willing and relaxed. Spring did cause us some concern, though, as she was slightly unsound. It wasn't something we'd noticed previously, but until now we'd really only worked her at a walk on flat surfaces so it wouldn't have been as obvious. Assuming that she was merely foot-sore from having short hooves and poor hoof balance, Amanda spent some time practising picking up her hooves so that she could be shod as soon as possible.

Now that Jackie and Spring were confident being ridden bareback, we

Top
Amanda and Spring riding through the river, three weeks out of the BLM yards.

Bottom
Red panicking in the fast-flowing water, moments before she lost her footing,
sending both horse and rider flying into the freezing water.

began introducing them to saddles. Jackie was uncomplicated, standing quietly to be saddled, and then trotted around the corral easily — having already accepted a person on her back, it seemed that the saddle was hardly something to worry her. However, Spring surprised us; although she hadn't been worried by the saddle blanket or a rider all week, this time she reared as soon as the surcingle was done up, and jumped over the rails from a standstill. With her now trapped inside the tie-up area we were unsure how to get her out, eventually having to get tools from the shed to unbolt the rails and lift them up so she could walk underneath.

Two days later — exactly four weeks after we'd collected the Mustangs from the BLM yards — we headed out for a trail ride. There were 'painted hills' on the Eastern Shoshone Indian Reservation, and we had permission to ride through the neighbouring ranch to get there. We set off in the freezing cold of the morning, expecting to be gone for a couple of hours. Amanda and Kirsty rode right from the outset, and once we were sure Spring was going well, I, too, mounted and rode alongside them, while Vicki and Alexa led their horses — both wearing surcingles. There were no fences to be seen in any direction, and as we scaled the steep hills we hoped our faith in them wasn't misplaced.

Spring still wasn't accepting a girth so Amanda was riding bareback, while Kirsty and I rode in saddles. All three were in rope halters — none of the horses would be ridden in bits until their teeth had been done by an equine dentist to avoid potential issues from wolf teeth (small premolars that interfere with a bit), retained caps (baby teeth that haven't fallen out, preventing the permanent teeth from coming through) or poorly aligned teeth. The occasional snowflake landed on us as we made our way deeper into the hills and a cold wind blew, causing us to snuggle deeper into our jackets. In contrast, Vicki and Alexa were shedding layers, kept warm by their strenuous hiking. They tied their discarded clothing to their horses — at first both horses were unsettled by the material flapping in the breeze, but within minutes they relaxed.

Finally we got to the painted hills, which had been a spectacular sight from the hills above with their marbled green and purple patterns. However, it was harder to see the colours once you were amongst them.

Alexa sitting on Coyote for the first time on day 22.

Top
Digit, Jackie and Spring on their first trail ride, three hours along riverbeds and up and down steep hills to get to the Painted Hills.

Bottom
Digit and Kirsty in the Painted Hills.

The type of soil was also different — the horses sank to their knees and we had to turn back to more solid ground and head for home. As we trotted up and down the hills, the horses were gaining confidence with every stride. They loved being out of the corrals and were in their element — incredibly sure-footed thanks to the hours of hiking we had done with them on the lead over the past two weeks.

Halfway home, Amanda pulled Spring up and jumped off to check one of the horse's legs. On the last hill she'd gone noticeably lame again and Amanda led her slowly the rest of the way. It was bad enough to warrant a vet to look over her, and we left her in the paddock to rest and recover while we worked out a plan.

Red was also causing Vicki to worry. Although she was fine being ridden at a walk, Vicki hadn't asked for more as Red was tight and uncomfortable through the neck, shoulders and withers and was showing symptoms of a horse in pain. If she turned too tightly it was like something was pinching her. She'd broncoed herself out of a Western saddle twice while being led at a walk, although she'd been relaxed in straight lines. She hadn't been ridden for the past week, instead Vicki focused on massaging the mare and doing skeletal work to improve her body, but she was still obviously sore. If we'd had her at home we would have turned her out to rest for several months, hoping that time off, followed by rehabilitation, would heal whatever damage had occurred. Without the luxury of the time to ensure that she was working with a pain-free horse, Vicki felt that Red was unsuited to a 100-day competition, and decided to get her seen by the vet also.

CONCERNED ABOUT RED'S AND SPRING'S SOUNDNESS, we called the BLM and the Mustang Heritage Foundation to discuss options. If the horses were vetted as unsuitable for ridden work and returned to the BLM yards within a few days, we could exchange them for other horses; trainers had up to 30 days to exchange unsuitable horses and that time was almost up.

As there were no equine vets in the area, we decided to get them looked at in Idaho, which also allowed us to be near the BLM yards to exchange horses if need be. It was already Friday and we had 10 hours of travel ahead of us, so we organised the vet check for Monday morning. It was rather an overwhelming concept, having to start from scratch if Red and Spring had to be swapped out — Vicki and Amanda would lose 30 days of training — but it was a very real possibility. Vicki had trained with a highly regarded team of farriers, vets and skeletal therapists, and was renowned for identifying and rehabilitating sore horses; if she believed that the horses were unfit for ridden work, then we were sure that the vets would only confirm our suspicions.

So, we were heading to Idaho on the assumption that two new wild horses would be joining the team and Red and Spring would be leaving us. Having become so emotionally attached to them, we began looking for wild horse sanctuaries where they could be re-homed and retired to pasture so that they wouldn't have to return to the BLM yards. We also rang ahead to see if we could base ourselves at Matt's property again — we would need his superior facilities to get our new Mustangs' handling started — and he was happy with that. Luckily we now had a new truck; as promised, the dealers who had sold us the first one had driven up from Idaho with another that was well suited to our needs.

Since we would be away for at least eight days, we had no choice but to take all of the Mustangs with us — we couldn't leave them for that long without handling, and there was no one at the dude ranch capable of looking after wild horses. The situation with the injured mares actually made us step out of our routine, and with Kirsty desperate to see the Grand Canyon we decided to make plans for a spontaneous road trip. Rather than returning to the dude ranch right away, we would travel down to Arizona with our horses and would be gone for at least a month. With limited space in both truck and trailer, we couldn't fit all of our luggage in, so left our town clothes behind — we'd be roughing it for much of the next four weeks anyway. We also left our winter clothes, as summer was approaching and we were heading down into desert country, so it could only get warmer.

With only the afternoon and the following morning left before we headed out, we had to pull out all the stops to get our Mustangs safe enough to handle and ride — especially Coyote, who was still miles behind the others. Having a difficult and unpredictable Mustang on the ranch was bad enough, without the added pressure of being on the road and riding through National Parks like we hoped to do in the coming weeks.

All of us now helped during Alexa's handling sessions. Coyote needed to learn to accept humans into her personal space and realise that they weren't there to hurt her. Normally we don't work to a deadline with our horses because some of them simply need more time, but as we were only on American soil for 100 days and could genuinely see hope for Coyote, we were prepared to adapt our normal way of doing things to make a breakthrough. We knew that if we gave up on her, she would go straight back to the BLM yards and have a lifetime of boredom ahead of her; alternatively, and even worse, as a 'second-strike' horse she would likely be re-homed to a rough-and-ready cowboy and be roped and thrashed into submission.

Determined to persevere, we started working her with a large ball to get her used to things being in her personal space, in the hope that she would become easier to handle. Initially, Alexa held her on the rope while the five of us kicked the ball to each other. Although the ball was never directed at her, Coyote was terrified of it and it took a firm hold from Alexa to keep her from fleeing. From this we progressed to playing soccer, and even though Coyote still considered the ball something to fear she soon learnt to face up to it, as she had to follow the ball every time Alexa turned to chase after it and kick it back to one of us. Soon Coyote was trotting and cantering on the lead after the ball while Alexa dribbled with it, only rearing or striking out if it accidently touched her.

By Saturday morning she had learnt to cope with the ball in motion; although she would tense when it brushed against her legs, she no longer tried to savage it when it got close. We now started bouncing the ball in front of her, then over her back, and slowly her tolerance for things in her personal space grew. While these methods were invasive, allowing the mare little option but to cope, it was neither traumatic nor painful for her in any way. She learnt that even things she feared didn't hurt her and, more importantly, that people were not as scary as she had once thought. From there she progressed to a saddle; instead of a rider, we bundled a tarpaulin up and laid it over the saddle, pulling it through the stirrups to keep it in place. By this point she had walked over and under the tarp and had had it all over her, so this wasn't stressful for her, and certainly much safer than using Alexa as a crash-test dummy.

We'd seen this method used by some of the other trainers in America, although it had been traumatising for their wild horses just days out of the BLM yards. With Coyote, it was a little different. By then she'd had a month of training and was used to wearing a surcingle, dragging things, walking over things and being lain over — we weren't overwhelming her with everything at once. She stood quietly while the tarp was secured to her saddle, then walked and trotted on the lead.

This gradual desensitisation hadn't been required by our other horses, but we hoped it would allow Coyote to take the next step. Since she was obviously unworried by the dummy on her back, Alexa decided it was time to hop on her, and she removed the tarp and slowly mounted. Keeping Coyote on the lead, so we could help if something went wrong, we circled the yard at a walk before having a small trot. The mare was coping well, and with less than 24 hours until we hit the road we led her out to the pasture to see how she would cope in an open area. Still keeping her on the lead, Alexa walked, trotted and cantered Coyote for the first time in the saddle before dismounting and giving her a huge pat. The mare was very relaxed — and for the first time since Alexa had first lain hands on her we had hopes that she had a chance at not only being ridden, but also being suitable for someone else to re-home after the Extreme Mustang Makeover.

With just 70 days to go, we were already 30 per cent of the way through our training; and Coyote, although significantly improved in some areas, was still a long way off from where she needed to be. Deciding to make the most of the ranch for one more ride, we delayed our departure until the following day so that we could have one final session with Coyote. Early on Sunday morning we rode the horses 30 minutes along the river, to work them on the flats on the neighbour's ranch. As Coyote showed more confidence when she had a leader, Vicki decided to ride one of the ranch horses and lead Coyote and Alexa.

This extra riding time was also invaluable for Jackie and me. I was hoping to have my first canter under saddle — I needed Jackie to be more advanced to go riding out with Coyote and two fresh Mustangs in the coming weeks; Jackie and Digit would have to be our lead horses and we needed them to be rock-solid. When working with wild horses back home in New Zealand, we have our experienced showjumpers to use as lead horses, and we knew how lucky we were to have Digit a step ahead of the others and able to offer confidence.

The ride started well, but Coyote panicked while crossing a river and started broncoing, rushing up behind Jackie and Digit — who fortunately held their ground. Vicki lost her grip on Coyote's lead and, as the mare spun, reared and then twisted with her head between her legs, Alexa fell. Although she hit the rocks on the far river bank, she bounced back up — bleeding from a bitten lip — caught the wayward mare and re-mounted. For the next 10 minutes, everything continued without disruption. Jackie and I slowly fell behind the others, who left the path to avoid a fallen log, weaving through the trees. Instead of following them, I asked Jackie to trot and aimed her for the log. She half-trotted, half-stumbled over it, not quite sure of what to do with her legs. It wasn't a bad effort for her first jump, though, and I smiled as I trotted to catch up with the other horses — but as they came back out onto the path, Coyote saw us approaching and was startled. Again she leapt sideways and reared before dropping her head and broncoing, and Alexa went flying. Feeling terrible, I slowed Jackie to a walk, and for the rest of the ride was careful to not jeopardise Alexa's safety by doing anything unexpected.

On reaching the flats, Vicki and Alexa headed to the far end so that there would be no distractions. Soon they were trotting, Coyote following closely behind the ranch horse. Kirsty and I trotted along the river's edge before weaving through the trees and finding small logs to jump. Both of the mares showed good technique once they got the hang of jumping, and pricked up their ears as they carefully navigated the natural obstacles. Vicki and Alexa joined us and watched as we approached a fallen tree —

at about 80 centimetres high, it was the biggest we'd attempted so far, but both Mustangs confidently jumped it and on landing Jackie cantered for the first time.

Circling back, we jumped it a few more times until Jackie was confidently cantering and turning. She was still quite reliant on following Digit, and I knew that once we got to Idaho it would be a priority to get her working independently. We would have to make sure that all of our Mustangs had turns as the lead horse, to ensure that they were confident in the front; and it was equally important that Digit, a natural leader, learnt to wait patiently and follow at the back.

Heading back, we purposely took a less-travelled path. Branches whipped at the horses' sides as we navigated the narrow trails, and we encouraged them to step over logs or through brushwood that had fallen over the path. Kirsty and I practised waving our arms and moving about in the saddle, getting our horses used to our hands and legs being everywhere — they were solid beneath us, and we were confident that they were exactly at the stage they needed to be before we headed off on our road trip.

After packing the last of our things and squeezing them into the vehicles, we caught Red and Spring and soon had the trailer hitched up to begin loading, knowing that this would be our last journey with the two bay mares. Both Vicki and Amanda had decided that neither of the horses could physically keep up with the workload required of them over the next 10 weeks. If they weren't vetted out and exchanged for new wild Mustangs for the challenge, Vicki and Amanda would withdraw. No amount of prize money would motivate either of them to compromise a horse's welfare and continue training it for an intensive competition when it was sore and not physically up to the challenge.

Top
Jackie's first time cantering and jumping, just four weeks from her wild state.

Bottom
Vicki leading Alexa and Coyote off one of the ranch horses.

CHAPTER 6

The end of the road

Red being trotted up for the vet back in Nampa, Idaho.

The drive to Idaho was surreal, back-tracking along the way we'd come only three weeks earlier. We had no real plans for the coming weeks — I'm sure we should have been more worried about this, but it was impossible not to feel some relief at being off the ranch. Any adventure was better than the repetition, isolation and boredom we had just been through.

We'd called ahead to ask the Livestock Commission in Twin Falls if we could keep our Mustangs in their yards again. Fortunately, they remembered us and were happy to help out again. Six hours later we pulled into the yards, unloaded the Mustangs, and the cowboys helped us settle them in. None of them could believe that these were the same wild horses that had stampeded and trampled us only weeks earlier; they all unloaded without trouble and walked calmly beside us as we made our way to the back yard. Reaching it, we slipped their halters off and let them loose — and instead of leaving us they waited around, happy to have our attention.

Once the horses were fed, we went in search of a Walmart store. The airline tickets, first truck and trailer, and keeping the horses fed and shod had already stretched our America budget, and having to spend a large amount extra to replace the truck had well and truly put us in the red. Now that we were on the road, our expenses would be significant — not only did we have the added cost of the diesel, but we also had to find somewhere for both ourselves and the horses to stay each night. After some thought we decided to rough it, so our first priority was to buy pillows, blankets and mattresses; luckily the weather was good, because there would undoubtedly be days to come when rain would make it impossible to sleep in the open-sided stock trailer.

Walmart's options were limited, but eventually we settled on one blanket and pillow each. The four others spent just US$15 each, but I decided to spoil myself and splashed out an extra US$3 on a thicker blanket — a decision I would come to appreciate hugely. Next we sought out towels, food and basic supplies, and after scouring the store for mattresses — with no luck — we bought two thin memory-foam pads for US$20 each.

We returned to the truck with our haphazard collection of camping supplies and went in search of somewhere to stay the night. We'd been told that the Shoshone Falls were stunning, so we headed there to watch the sunset. The cascading waterfalls were even better than we had expected, and we scrambled over rocks to see marmots and hiked along several trails. We'd bought wraps for dinner; the food was good, and with darkness now upon us we decided it would be gorgeous to wake up to the roar of the waterfalls, so settled down for the night in the car park. It quickly got cold, and with limited blankets and a decidedly hard bed I jumped in the truck to sleep on the back seat, hoping it would be more comfortable. I'd just drifted off when a knock woke me, and I opened my eyes to the blinding light of a torch. Startled and disorientated, I sat up to find a man watching me through the window; it took several seconds before I grasped what he was saying, and I looked a little closer at what he was wearing to confirm that he was a sheriff like he claimed.

Realising we were breaking the law, essentially by becoming vagrants, I quickly apologised, promised to relocate and climbed through to the driver's seat before realising I had no idea how to drive with a trailer on. Mortified I jumped out, opened the door of the trailer and whispered for Vicki to wake up; half-asleep, she nodded to the law officer before starting the engine and navigating the steep, winding road leading away from the waterfall. After driving around in the dark for 30 minutes and finding nowhere suitable to park the truck, we stopped in a rest area at the side of the road; it was well after midnight and we were all desperate for sleep. As we were parked on a slight slope in front of a huge cliff, Vicki shook Kirsty awake and told her to find some rocks to put under the wheels, in case the brakes failed, before falling into bed again.

The next morning we woke at sunrise, hoping to get away before the sheriff found us again. It had been a freezing and uncomfortable night, and Amanda had ended up sleeping on the wooden floor of the trailer with the mattress on top of her for added warmth — not a promising start. We had the Mustangs caught and loaded by 7 a.m. and got on the road. It took less than three hours to reach the vet clinic in Nampa, and we arrived in plenty of time for our appointment. Red and Spring were unloaded while the rest waited on the trailer, and soon the vets joined us. They were all impressed by how quiet the Mustangs were to handle after just a month of training, and quickly began assessing the horses. Spring was slightly unsound when turning, but hoof testers showed no signs of an abscess in the hoof. However, X-rays revealed the severity of her issues — her fetlock (the hinge joint just above the hoof) showed an old fracture and extensive calcification. It was even worse than we had feared and there was no chance of improvement — Spring was unsuited to ridden work in any capacity. Red, too, was vetted out; the vets called the BLM and began drafting a letter detailing their diagnosis.

Although Vicki and Amanda had been sure the horses weren't 100 per cent, they were disheartened to have their fears confirmed. And now, with 30 days gone, the process of taming a wild horse would begin again. One of the vets called us inside to talk to a representative at the Mustang Heritage Foundation, and I listened to what they said in shock: today marked 31 days since the Mustangs had been assigned to trainers, and as they had a 30-day swap-out policy the Foundation wasn't prepared to let Vicki and Amanda have new Mustangs to train for the competition. When I explained that we'd discussed this with them a few days earlier and today was the earliest we'd been able to get an appointment, due to the weekend, they apologised but wouldn't reconsider their stand on the matter.

Vicki and Amanda were dumbfounded when I told them, and the rest of us were equally disappointed — we'd spent tens of thousands of dollars to come to America to tame Mustangs and help change the negative stereotypes these horses have, in the hope of inspiring people to re-home them from the BLM yards — and now our best two riders were out of the competition. Without a decent finish in the Extreme Mustang Makeover, our credibility was shot. Alexa and Kirsty were only competing for the fun of it, and I, as the least experienced of the three sisters, had never expected to do as well — it was always Vicki and Amanda who we'd had high hopes for. Of the five of us, they were the only professional riders and really had the best chance of not only producing a Mustang to a superior level of training but also delivering

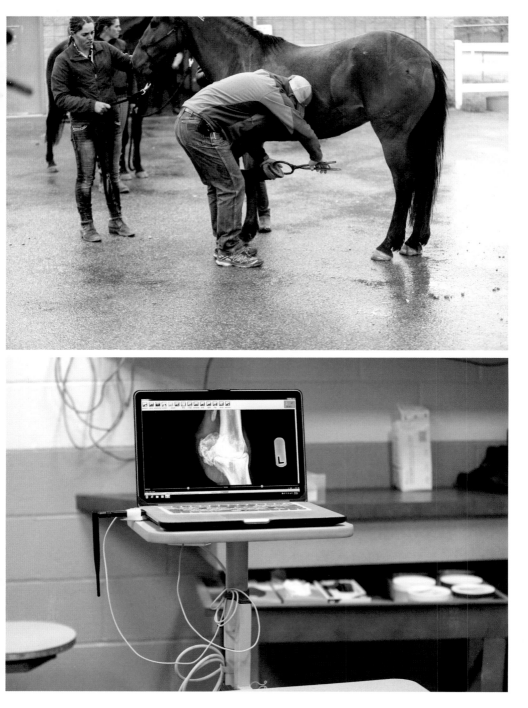

Top
The vet checking Spring with hoof testers for possible causes of her lameness.

Bottom
Spring's X-rays showed an old fracture to her fetlock on her left foreleg.

a polished performance in the competition arena. Red and Spring had been coming along so well, and it was hugely disappointing that the time and love Vicki and Amanda had invested into their Mustangs had been for nothing.

Loading the horses back into the trailer we set off to Matt's. It was a long and sombre drive as we mulled over our options and thought about just how much this affected our plans. Amanda glanced at me with a smile, sympathetically saying 'No pressure, but you're the only Wilson sister left in this competition', and I felt all the pressure. I had never anticipated making it into the top 10, and knew that with Vicki and Amanda sidelined, there would be bigger expectations of Alexa, Kirsty, and especially me, in the coming months.

VICKI AND AMANDA HAVE NEVER BEEN ONES for being knocked down by adversity, and being out of the competition didn't mean that their days taming wild Mustangs were over. After settling our horses in at Matt's we set off for the BLM yards. There were 50,000 Mustangs in captivity across the country, and if we could offer a couple of them a good start to domesticated life, it would be worth it. Not only would it allow Vicki and Amanda to have horses to ride over the next few months, but also, as we were to find out, it would reveal the great differences in the horses available for adoption.

Although Red or Spring were now essentially useless, we didn't leave our beautiful mares in the BLM yards. We had offered them a taste of freedom and were desperately trying to find a place where they could be retired to pasture in a herd situation, although so far we hadn't had much success with the Mustang sanctuaries scattered across the West. Not willing to give up yet, though, we were keeping them with us until all options were exhausted; so, the two new additions would bring our numbers up to seven, however temporarily.

The BLM yards at Boise had 100 Mustangs on-site and the staff led us from yard to yard, introducing us to the horses available for adoption. They could recognise most on sight, and recall their ages and Herd Management Areas, and we were impressed by the care and passion they had for the wild horses in their charge. At the pen of adult mares, the staff pointed out the two replacement Extreme Mustang Makeover mares we would have been assigned. One was a rangy bay mare from Jackies Butte that had been mustered at the same time as Jackie, and the other was the black mare Vicki had originally been assigned, with the back and hoof problems. Neither impressed us, and since we had the luxury of choosing our new Mustangs, as they wouldn't be competing, we stood at the rails watching them all for a while.

The EMM mares drifted to the back of the pen, wary; a few other horses held their ground, and the more curious ones wandered up to the fence and stopped several feet away. A stunning bay mare caught our eye and we pointed her out. Steve, the manager, shook his head and said he wouldn't recommend her — the six-year-old was a one-strike horse that had developed a rearing issue with her trainer. Always up for a challenge, Vicki wasn't about to be put off — this was by far the classiest horse in the pen — and continued asking questions, but Steve said that if it had been any other trainer he could have lain some of the blame on him, but this guy had trained plenty of Mustangs and if he'd given up on this one, she must have had some serious behavioural issues.

Undecided, we continued on to the next yard. This was a smaller area, with each Mustang kept separate. In the first pen a stunning eight-year-old mare with unique flaxen sorrel colouring caught Vicki's eye. She also was a one-strike Mustang, having been started and returned by a young girl unable to commit to the costs involved with owning a horse. Steve reminded us that adopting a one-strike horse only cost US$25, as opposed to US$150 for a completely untrained one. There were still plenty of other horses to look at, so we continued on. Passing over a recently mustered eight-year-old gelding, partly because of a swelling on his front leg, but also because having a recently gelded herd stallion among our mares was asking for trouble, we moved on. The next pen contained a selection of quality geldings between three and four years old, and we stood by the rail for several minutes to watch them. A golden palomino stood out — he was the only one in the right age group that had any colour — but it was his conformation, kind eyes and curious

Of the 120 Mustangs we saw at the Boise
yards on our second visit, these two
geldings caught our eye. We re-homed
them as part of the TIP program and
named them Gunnar and Deacon.

nature that won us over. Wandering over, he stood watching us closely, and when Vicki reached through the fence he sniffed her outstretched fingers; the only horse that had attempted to make human contact. Steve explained that, despite never having left the BLM yards, this four-year-old was also technically a one-strike horse and available for US$25 — someone had paid an adoption fee but never collected him.

With Vicki enamoured with her palomino, it was now Amanda's turn to choose. Heading back, we looked through all of the pens again and made a short-list of our favourites, but eventually she turned to us and said she'd pick the first Mustang that walked up to the fence and let her touch it, assuming that it was sound and had half-decent conformation. Laughing, we agreed that this wasn't a bad plan, and Amanda sat on the fence waiting to be chosen. None of the mares were brave enough to initiate contact, not even the one-strike horses that had previously been handled, and nor were the older geldings. Amanda returned to the pen containing Vicki's palomino and sat waiting, and like bees to a honey pot the horses began making their way over to her. The first to arrive was a sorrel, and he stood still while she trailed her fingers over his outstretched head. When the other Mustangs saw the attention he was getting they crept closer, and soon a handful stood to be touched. Initially they flinched and moved off when our hands brushed against them, but soon returned and eventually stood still to enjoy the contact.

Amanda was quite taken with her inquisitive sorrel, and we asked more about him. He was a three-year-old that had been born in the BLM yards, and had recently been seen by the vet because he often had his tongue sticking out and at times accidently bit it. The vet had assured the BLM that the gelding was just bored, and that being re-homed to a more stimulating environment would hopefully reduce the trait. We asked to see the horses moving, to check for soundness issues, and one of the staff jumped the fence and got the horses trotting for us so we could look for any unevenness in their gaits.

Both the palomino and the sorrel looked sound, and the process of re-homing them began.

CHAPTER 7

New experiences

Just five days out of the Boise Wild Horse Corrals, Amanda and Deacon were cantering out over thousands of acres of BLM land.

Top
Gunnar being sorted at the BLM yards.

Bottom
Amanda and Deacon just minutes after he had been unloaded — his first time being touched.

Re-homing wasn't entirely straightforward. While the horses waited on the trailer, we set to work filling out paperwork; the manager had realised that we couldn't adopt the horses because we'd have to maintain ownership of them for 12 months, which clearly wasn't possible with us leaving the country 70 days later. Instead, BLM arranged for us to train the horses as part of the Trainer Incentive Program (TIP); basically, we had to get the horses handled, able to be caught, picking up all four feet and loading onto a trailer, and then find them a permanent home. To cover the time and cost of getting the horses out of the BLM yards and to that stage in their training, the government would pay us US$750–800 per horse. Since they remained the property of the BLM, we weren't able to sell them; instead, they had to be adopted out for just US$150, even though we planned to get our two TIP horses working under saddle.

We were thankful just to have the opportunity to take on two more horses, and soon had the paperwork completed. The process of taming wild horses was about to begin again and we were relieved to see how excited Vicki and Amanda were — what had started out as a disappointing day had quickly become full of promise. On the drive back to the ranch we brainstormed names, settling on Gunnar for the palomino and Deacon for the sorrel — named after country singers on our favourite TV show. The names were very fitting, as country music was the only thing we'd listened to since arriving in the Wild West and we'd developed quite an appreciation for it.

Gunnar and Deacon were far more settled than our mares had been, and Vicki and Amanda were able to clip ropes onto their halters. Rather than running the horses down to the yards, they kept hold of the ropes and led them. Both horses were confused by the pressure on their halters and tossed their heads, but with a little patience they soon understood what was being asked. Although it was nearly sunset, Vicki and Amanda got to work befriending their Mustangs while Alexa, Kirsty and I started feeding and mucking out the rest of the horses. I watched their progress out of the corner of my eye: these boys definitely weren't as wary as the EMM mares had been a month earlier, which was a relief — by choosing horses that had a natural curiosity about humans, they had saved significant time in training.

Within half an hour, both horses could lead back and forth in the race, and be touched over most of the body. Vicki even called Alexa over to hold Gunnar while she jumped up and down beside his shoulder, eventually lying over his back while he stood waiting. This wild Mustang had only been out of the BLM yards for two hours, yet was at the same stage as our mares had been after two weeks.

Beyond satisfied with the horses' progress, we headed inside for dinner. It was clear that the EMM mares were not an accurate example of the Mustangs available for adoption; although it was devastating that Red and Spring had injuries, this had given us the opportunity to return to the yards and re-home additional horses, something we wouldn't have done otherwise. Matt had told us at the outset that the EMM mares were those least likely to be re-homed: horses of plainer colour, more recently mustered or a little flightier — basically, the horses most likely to require professional trainers to get them started under saddle. Our EMM mares were most like the wild Kaimanawas straight off the range — needing a lot more time, patience and expertise to win over — but our two new Mustangs were more like unhandled stationbreds you would find in rural areas of New Zealand: purpose-bred horses managed in paddocks, but left to run in herds and essentially untouched until old enough to be started under saddle.

THE NEXT MORNING VICKI AND AMANDA WOKE EARLY, excited to see how receptive their new horses would be, and hopeful that they would be as willing as yesterday; Vicki was sure that Gunnar was ready for his first ride. Starting from scratch, they caught the horses, brushed them all over (something we'd only been able to do with the mares after a week of handling) and were soon lying over their backs again; Vicki on Gunnar for the second time, and Amanda on Deacon for the first. Both horses were enjoying the attention and, by the looks of it, were thrilled to have a change of scenery. They tackled everything being asked of them with a cheeky look, and within 20 minutes both Vicki and Amanda were sitting astride on their horses; happy to sit there, they chatted for half an hour while the two geldings ate the hay in their yards, completely unconcerned.

That afternoon, Vicki led Gunnar into the round pen and got on him bareback, first teaching him to move forward off the leg and turn to the lightest aids on the halter. Soon they were trotting around in circles, walking over tarpaulins and investigating the camera that Amanda was filming them with. Ready for a bigger area, I opened the gate to let Vicki ride out into the Western arena, walking slowly around the edges to let the curious gelding say hello to the ranch horses over the fence.

Amanda wasn't quite so brave, and led Deacon on foot to join them. The young gelding wanted to join Gunnar and didn't appreciate being held back on a rope. When he tugged on the lead rope Amanda blocked his attempts to escape; annoyed, Deacon reared and tried to spin away. Again Amanda turned him back. She waited for him to settle, but he continued to work himself up, tossing his head and rearing, before turning and trying to drag Amanda after him. When he realised he couldn't do what he wanted, he completely threw his toys out of the cot — stomping his forelegs in anger like a spoilt child before throwing himself to the ground in a temper tantrum. Unable to control her hysterics, Amanda burst out laughing at his childish antics, and Vicki and Kirsty, who was on Digit, rode over to watch the young gelding.

Now that he was on the ground, in the sand, he made the most of it and rolled before leaping to his feet and repeating it all over again. Three times he threw himself to the ground, annoyed that he still couldn't follow Gunnar, but finally he stood up, yawned in boredom and stood quietly beside Amanda while she patted him. These two boys had the most unusual personalities — with traits most likely arising from years of boredom in the yards — and we couldn't wait to see what comical mischief they would get up to next.

The next day, less than 48 hours since they had been collected from the BLM yards, our two latest arrivals progressed to being ridden in saddles. For Gunnar this was a natural progression from his earlier rides, but due to our looming deadline — it was almost time for us to leave on our road trip — Amanda decided to bypass some of the bareback stages

Top
Vicki and Gunnar's second ride, fewer than 24 hours out of the BLM yards.

Bottom
Deacon throwing a tantrum because he couldn't follow Gunnar, who was being ridden.

and have her first proper ride with a saddle. If she could get Deacon cantering in the arena today, she would be able to take him out on the trails before we headed off to ride in the unknown.

Although Deacon had now been saddled a couple of times, Amanda took nothing for granted, first sitting on him bareback before saddling him and lying over the saddle. Up to this point he had just stood, or taken the occasional step, while Amanda had sat on him. Today would be his first time trotting and, hopefully, if everything went well, cantering. Vicki rode Diamond, Matt's winning Mustang from the 2012 Extreme Mustang Makeover, into the ring to work alongside Amanda. Once Amanda was in the saddle and Deacon was confidently walking, Vicki asked Diamond to trot, in the hope that this would encourage Deacon to increase his pace. Unsettled, Amanda begged her to stop, but Vicki reminded her that it was better to establish the basics now, while we had access to good facilities, rather than risk it going wrong on the open trails. Amanda nodded grimly, held on tight and slowly forced herself to relax into the saddle. For the next few minutes she would essentially be a dummy so that the horse could get accustomed to the feel and weight of a rider; the directions and speed were being set by Vicki, who again urged Diamond into a trot.

Following willingly, Deacon trotted behind Diamond, and since he appeared relaxed Vicki increased the pace again and Deacon cantered to keep up. The young gelding, intent on his task, changed tempo and beneath Amanda his paces were relaxed and even. Normally, if a young horse is going to panic or react negatively when first ridden in a saddle, it will do so in the change of pace; with the scariest part behind her, Amanda's look of concentration was quickly replaced by a widening smile. Relaxing further into the saddle, she readjusted her seat and settled down to enjoy the ride. The next few minutes were spent accustoming the horse to listen to cues from his rider, as opposed to Vicki, and, although confused at first, Deacon soon learnt the very basics of stopping and turning. Thrilled with his progress, Amanda swung down from the saddle, gave him a reassuring pat and led him over to his yard to rest.

Although it had felt like a lifetime, the ride had taken less than

15 minutes. Vicki swapped Diamond for a fresh horse, this time riding Dan — Matt's winning horse from the 2014 Extreme Mustang Makeover — and waited for Alexa to saddle Coyote. They'd worked the cantankerous mare off the horse the day before, and, like at the dude ranch, Coyote had seemed more relaxed with a leader. Because the mare still wasn't reliable enough to put a rider straight on, Vicki got her walking, trotting and cantering on the lead before trusting her enough to allow Alexa to mount. We'd never had to do as much preventative work in over 15 years of training, but Alexa was practically family and we valued her life too much to trust her to a mare who seemed hell-bent on throwing her rider at every turn.

Satisfied that Coyote was now ready, Alexa was legged up into the saddle and waited for Vicki to re-mount. Wanting to keep the mare's mind busy, Vicki urged Dan into a trot, keeping a firm hold on the rope while Alexa kept her body relaxed and her hold on the halter reins as loose as possible. Dan was well trained and performed accurate sliding halts, halt to canters and rein-backs at the lightest touch; and Coyote, who was now used to staying with her shadow, quickly followed the other horse's movements and was soon mimicking basic Western moves.

Twenty minutes into the session, just as everyone had relaxed, thinking that Coyote had finally had a breakthrough, the unpredictable mare reared and leapt sideways, throwing Alexa violently to the ground — her seventh fall in as many days. Rising gingerly to her feet, she re-approached the mare, and Vicki dismounted to help her back into the saddle. They resumed where they'd left off, and for the next 10 minutes Coyote didn't put a foot wrong. She'd had a solid 30-minute workout with only one instance when she forgot herself; it was a huge improvement on previous rides, especially considering the advanced moves asked of her and the number of transitions she'd done.

AT THE DINNER TABLE THAT NIGHT, we asked Matt and Stacie if they'd be able to take us for a ride to see herds of wild Mustangs — they'd mentioned it when we had first stayed, and we thought it was too good an opportunity to miss out on. While they were more than

willing, they said they didn't have enough ranch horses for all of us to ride. Laughing, we said that we were planning to ride our Mustangs — and there was dead silence at the table as they looked at us to see if we were joking. They had been watching us working the horses on the arena, and knew that two of the Mustangs had only been ridden in a saddle once, Coyote hadn't been ridden off a lead, and Jackie had only learnt to canter independently the day before. Digit was still the most advanced, and of all the horses she was the one we were confident would be the easiest out on the trails.

We spent the next 10 minutes assuring Matt and Stacie that we'd be fine; I think we were trying to convince ourselves more than anything. Soon it was agreed that we would head out to see the wild horses in the Hardtrigger Wild Horse Management Area, riding out from the Wilson Creek trailhead two days later. The only risk was that if we fell off, our Mustangs would be loose in 80,000 hectares of BLM land, and none of them were saints to catch yet.

With one last day to prepare both ourselves and the horses, we saddled up the next morning and headed out for a ride through the BLM land that bordered the ranch. Jackie and Digit had been out on the trails the day before, and were bold and brave at the front. Vicki was again on Dan, leading Coyote and Alexa, and Amanda followed closely behind on a ranch horse. It was a huge ask to trust Coyote in such wide-open spaces and we weren't entirely convinced that she was ready for it — but if she managed to behave today, Alexa was game enough to take her out in search of wild horses.

Not wanting any of the horses to develop a preference for either leading or following, we constantly changed the order as we rode along. At first Digit objected to having to trail behind and Jackie was hesitant at the front, but gradually they adjusted — both mares were confident, calm and able to be ridden on a long rein. They had progressed from halters to bosals (a Western-style bridle with no bit), and from bareback to English saddles to Western saddles, and were proving to be very versatile. Vicki had returned from a closing-down sale the day before with an assortment of gear, including three Western saddles and a stock saddle so that we could all ride out at the same time without anyone having to go bareback or ruin a jumping saddle — these were worth thousands of dollars as opposed to the hundreds she'd spent on the clearance stock. Although the quality of the leather was only average, the saddles sat well on the horses; this was vital — we would rather ride bareback than put our horses in gear that would pinch them and make ridden life a discomfort.

Deciding our relaxed ride wasn't enough of a test for tomorrow, Vicki took the lead. She urged Dan into a canter and Coyote changed pace to keep up. Soon we were flying along a sunken motorbike track, navigating winding turns and dodging discarded tyres and shrubs as the miles fell away behind us. Occasionally we'd fall back to a trot or walk to rest the horses, but our mares were quite fit by now.

Heading for home, we found a sandy track and Vicki unclipped Coyote from her lead. Telling Alexa, Kirsty and me to keep up, Vicki cantered off with Amanda, leaving us in their dust. We looked at each other, shrugged and gave our Mustangs their heads — and quickly caught up. We were almost on top of them when the two ranch horses checked mid-stride and executed perfect sliding stops on the sandy track. Unprepared for this sudden change in pace we flew past them, halting a few metres ahead. Shaking her head, Vicki told us to try a little harder, and again the ranch horses cantered off and we followed. This time we kept a watchful eye on Vicki and Amanda, and when we saw them shift their bodies back we mimicked it, preparing our horses to gather their hindquarters. When they halted we stopped just behind them, their horses acting as a natural barrier. Our Mustangs were effectively stopping in response to body language, and, by following the other horses' lead, without us having to apply any pressure to their reins.

Over the next 20 minutes we continued these actions, and Coyote, who was well used to it after her session on the arena the day before, was by far the best. But even Kirsty's and my black mares were quickly getting the hang of the canter-to-halt transitions and by the end of the ride were very consistent. If we were impressed with our horses after five weeks out of the BLM yards and less than 10 rides, though, we were about to have our pride dented by Gunnar, who was next to be ridden out on the trail with ranch horses. He cantered down the tracks like a pro — at the same stage in his training, in just a tenth of the time, as Jackie and Digit.

Deacon still had to go out, and Vicki joined Amanda in the pasture on a ranch horse. It was their first ride outside the arena and Amanda was a little nervous. Deacon didn't seem like the type of horse to be ill-meaning, but the pasture contained plenty of obstacles to distract a young animal with no life experience. Having been born in the BLM yards, three-year-old Deacon had never been off flat ground or been exposed to anything much, but Amanda didn't have to worry. He was curious and brave by nature, and so thankful to have a job to do that he was eager to please and boldly followed behind the ranch horse; first trotting, then cantering, lengths of the field, although at times he did round his back playfully, his head low as he tossed it in enjoyment. Satisfied with the young gelding on just his second ride, Amanda gave him a pat and dismounted. It was a great finish, and, although she hadn't pushed enough buttons to trust him on the big ride tomorrow and would borrow a ranch horse instead, she was happy with his progress.

The last thing we needed to do in preparation for the ride was get the horses shod. All five horses were due at the equine dentist later that afternoon, and since the vet would be there to sedate them, Vicki decided to shoe the horses at the same time. Coyote wasn't yet ready for shoeing, but Jackie, Digit and Gunnar were good about having their front and their back hooves picked up. Shoeing would benefit them greatly, both on the rocky terrain tomorrow and on our road trip. The horses behaved well during the dental work and the shoeing. By the time they returned to full consciousness, they were looking like show ponies; as we had also clipped their bridle paths and legs, their transformation from wild to domesticated was impossible to miss.

Early the next morning, we saddled the Mustangs before we loaded them on the trailer — there were no yards or fences where we were headed, just vast areas of range land, so the less risk of the horses getting loose the better. We were soon on our way: our four Mustangs loaded in the trailer and three ranch horses being driven separately, one for Amanda and the other two for Matt and Stacie. An hour later we pulled

Top
Gunnar's first ride out on the trails, three days out of the BLM yards; the first time he had ever been off flat ground or outside an enclosed space.

Bottom
Jackie being shod for the first time, after 34 days of handling.

into the car park at the Wilson Creek trailhead, and one at a time we unloaded our Mustangs. The car park was surrounded with signs about the risks of riding among wild horses, warning riders not to ride mares in the area . . . it wasn't encouraging. Before Alexa mounted, Matt led Coyote off his ranch horse, cantering the mare around the car park to ensure that she was ready to ride. Soon, Vicki, Alexa, Kirsty and I were on our Mustangs, and beside us Amanda was attempting to mount her grey ranch gelding while holding her film camera — she was anticipating a disastrous ride and didn't want to miss out on the unfolding drama. On the off-chance that we fell off and a Mustang galloped off over the horizon, Amanda joked that we could need footage to explain how we lost one of our horses.

Matt and Stacie swung into their saddles, turned their horses and cantered down the track; as they were our only guides, it was worrying to watch them disappear down the path. Our Mustangs were still very inexperienced, and in such wide-open spaces we'd planned to warm them up slowly. Shrugging at the change in plan, Vicki spun Gunnar around, gave him his head and cantered off to catch up; although it was only his fourth ride, he was responsive and confident. Looking back over her shoulder, Vicki called out for us to 'keep up and hang on' — and with little choice, we picked up to a canter as we followed after the disappearing riders. I was sure we were being tested, and with so much potential for things to go wrong I really hoped that luck would stay on our side and none of us would hit the dirt.

Glancing over my shoulder at Coyote, I saw Alexa give me a reassuring smile and assumed that her mare felt relaxed. I settled into the saddle to enjoy my own ride; Jackie was feeling better than ever. Sometimes we followed the sandy tracks, and sometimes we went across country, weaving between cactus flowers, boulders and shrubs. The horses were nimble and sure-footed; and, most importantly, they were enjoying themselves. As we rode deeper into the heart of the BLM land, we came across a steep decline and wound our way down, zigzagging along a narrow track before dropping down to a river flowing between two towering cliffs. Hugging the edges of the rock walls, we rode along a

Top
Our truck and trailer, laden with horses.

Bottom
Jackie and I taking turns riding away from the other horses — it was remarkable
how much we could trust these wild horses after just five weeks of handling.

narrow rock ledge, the lush green grass of the valley floor a stark contrast to the desert-like conditions up top.

With our curiosity satisfied, we turned around and rode back out to continue our search for wild horses. Up and down hills we rode, some so steep that Jackie was in danger of losing her Western saddle over her head, and I had to dismount and lead her. Once, someone ahead called out that they'd spotted a rattlesnake and I climbed back onto Jackie in a panic, feeling sure I would be safer well off the ground. Gingerly riding past, I kept a wary eye on the lethal predator; during the next 10 minutes we passed several more.

Soon we dropped down into another river, with thick scrub bordering the water's edge. To save back-tracking, we bashed our way through the tangled branches, hugging our horses' necks to avoid getting caught up as they leapt the fast-flowing water. Safely on the other side, we cantered to the horizon before winding along a steep switchback. So far we'd been riding for two hours and there were no signs of wild horses. Still keen to see the herds, we circled back a different way, navigating up and down hills as we headed home. With vast expanses of land and no Mustangs in sight, we spent the last part of our ride training our horses to work independently, taking turns to ride away from the group and out of sight before returning to join the others.

Three hours into the ride, Gunnar quit on Vicki and lay down to rest — the young gelding had only been out of the BLM corrals for five days now, and was not conditioned to cover so much ground. Although the majority of the ride had been at the walk, the undulating terrain was tiring for a horse used to being confined on flat ground. Fortunately, we were almost back at the trailer, and after a rest he was refreshed and ready for the final stretch.

Shortly afterwards we stopped to water the horses at the long concrete toughs the BLM had installed so that the wild horses had something to drink even in the hottest of summers when water was in scarce supply. Once they'd drunk their fill, we wound up the final hill before making our way back to the trailer. Although there'd been no wild horses in sight, it had been an eventful ride and the Mustangs had impressed us at every turn.

Top
Alexa and Coyote's second time off the lead during our ride at Wilson Creek.

Bottom
Kirsty and Digit at Wilson Creek, just 39 days out of the BLM yards.

CHAPTER 8

NZ Ranch

High up in the mountains, deep in the heart of the Eagle Cap Wilderness in Oregon, we came across an iced-over waterfall and had to turn back on a narrow and rocky ledge.

The morning after our ride in the open country, we decided to say farewell to Matt and Stacie and set off to Oregon. Just two hours' drive away was NZ Ranch, which was owned by one of the vets, Liz, who had checked Red and Spring over at the clinic. She'd married a Kiwi and we were looking forward to meeting a fellow New Zealander.

Even without an address we would have recognised the ranch as soon as we saw the entrance — it was the first time since being in America that we'd seen normal fencing, and as we drove past irrigated paddocks filled with crops on one side and sheep on the other, we experienced a feeling of nostalgia. It was just like being on a station in our home country, and we reminisced about everything we missed — good fencing, green grass and the taste of New Zealand water were the things we missed the most about home.

The turnaround outside the house was roughly fenced with waratahs, sheep-netting and a crude shelter for orphan lambs made from sheets of iron, not dissimilar to farms across much of New Zealand. Feeling so much at home, we wandered over to pat the baa-ing lambs who playfully bunted us. Behind us someone called out in greeting, and spinning around we couldn't contain our smiles. Bob might have lived in America for years, but he obviously visited New Zealand often — his accent was as Kiwi as they come, and it felt good hearing the familiar sound.

Unloading the Mustangs, we led them into the barn to be stabled. They were curious about the sheep, and hung their heads out of the window to watch the smaller animals graze. One curious lamb ran over and stood on its hind legs trying to reach Deacon, who lurched backwards. Regaining his courage, he peered out the window again and the lamb leapt up a second time. Confused, Deacon stood there watching the boisterous creature for a while before returning to his hay.

With the horses sorted for the night, we settled down to unpack and make ourselves comfortable in the guest cabin, as we were staying for a few days. Soon, Liz arrived home and welcomed us with open arms; although we'd met her only briefly at the vet clinic, it felt like we'd been reunited with an old friend and we headed into the house to talk while dinner was being made. Even the meal was reminiscent of New Zealand, and we had a lovely evening sharing stories and getting to know each other properly.

The next morning dawned clear, and eager to help out we rounded up the cattle in the lower fields to bring the calves in for branding. The horses started off quite wobbly; they were unsure about approaching the cattle and about having to work parallel with each other to keep the animals moving. Digit (unsurprisingly) was the boldest, and Jackie and Gunnar soon got the hang of it, but Coyote remained unsure, half-following as we got the cattle moving in the right direction. Up on the driveway Amanda was filming our efforts, and once she'd got enough footage she mounted Deacon, who was fussing at having to stay behind, and quickly trotted across to meet us.

Once the cattle were in the yards we sorted them, bringing them into a smaller yard. Hitching our Mustangs to the rails, we set to work separating the calves and pushing them down a chute to be freeze-branded, drenched and given injections. Each of us had a turn at branding, and several calves sported a messed-up and barely recognisable 'NZ' on the shoulder from our early attempts at holding the branding iron in place. Once all of the calves were done, we mounted and herded them back to pasture, before returning to the barn to unsaddle and wash off the horses and let them out in the paddock to graze with the sheep.

Late that afternoon we set out on foot, hiking to the edge of the boundary fence and crossing over onto neighbouring land. At an abandoned colonial house, in disrepair, Liz shared the history of the area as we poked through the dust and under floorboards in search of clues to the pioneers who had once lived there. Loose pages of old schoolbooks and newspapers from the early 1900s gave hints that the house had stood empty for almost 100 years, but it wasn't until we found a letter between lovers that we really began to piece together what life had been like for its inhabitants a century earlier. Fascinated, we spent ages unfolding fragile pages, looking for more handwritten letters. Finally, with the sun setting, we drifted outside to peek in the old outhouse, feed shed and chicken

coop before walking back home. Along the way we spotted mushrooms and picked them, thinking that they would be the perfect addition to our bacon and eggs the following morning.

THE NEXT DAY WE HEADED OFF EARLY, loading the horses into the trailer to drive to Liz and Bob's summer pasture on Ironside Mountain. It was 12 miles (20 kilometres) down the gravel road, and we had plans to spend the day riding the perimeter, checking on stock and keeping an eye out for damaged fences, with a break for a picnic lunch. Liz and Bob were coming along to fence and had drawn us a rough map to follow, since they wouldn't be riding out over the 3000 acres with us. I was given the honour of directing our way. As we rounded the first hill there was a fork in the path; unsure of which direction to take, I pulled the map from my pocket and opened it up, startling Jackie who leapt sideways and slid down the steep embankment. I dropped the map as I scrambled frantically for the reins.

Ignoring the others laughing on the path above me, I dismounted, retrieved the crumpled map from the ground and led Jackie back up the hill to pass it to Kirsty. Digit was far more relaxed about the unfamiliar rustling noise, and stood while Kirsty orientated herself. Confident that she had a reasonable idea of the direction we were headed in, we set off in search of cattle, counting them as we went. Easily distracted by the scenery we frequently detoured, weaving our way up and down the steep countryside as we covered mile after mile.

After getting a little lost after detouring to scale a rocky outcrop, we scrambled up a shale hill, the loose rock moving beneath the horses' hooves, until it got so steep we had to get off and lead them. At the top we paused to let the horses graze before re-mounting and riding down an equally steep hill on the other side. In the valley below we found a herd of cattle, and a quick count determined that at least half of the stock we were searching for had now been found. Turning, we rode up another hill in search of the rest. As we cantered along, Jackie jumped a sagebrush instead of dodging it, and since jumping is notoriously hard in a Western saddle I was dislodged and fell hard. Getting stiffly to my feet, I watched my startled mare draw to a stop 100 metres away and I set off towards her, the other riders circling back to join me. Ahead, Jackie turned and cantered further away; after instructing the others not to follow, I turned and went after her. Still eluding me she cantered off again, this time crossing the ridge-line and disappearing out of sight. In annoyance I trailed after her, but when I got to the top she was nowhere to be seen. Hoping she had stayed on the track, I continued walking and calling her, pausing when I heard the pounding of hooves. Jackie galloped around a bend and came to a halt just metres in front of me. Talking softly, I took a step towards her to take hold of the reins, but again she spun and cantered off out of sight.

Frustrated, sore and tired, I followed in the direction she'd disappeared. For the next 30 minutes, the black mare moved like a shadow — I would catch glimpses of her as she crossed ridge-lines or wove through trees, but every time I reached the place I'd last seen her she was long gone. I was thankful she was only loose in a 3000-acre paddock; I could only imagine the disaster if one of us had fallen off a few days before on the BLM land.

Almost at the point of giving up, I began wandering aimlessly, at this point completely unsure where Jackie had gone. It was with huge relief when I saw Kirsty cantering over the hill towards me; her mare, worried about having come so far alone, neighed loudly. Jackie was obviously within hearing distance, because she suddenly appeared on the skyline at a gallop, making her way down to us at a breakneck speed. Halting beside Digit, she stood quietly; but as I walked up to her she circled away, and in the end Kirsty had to ride up and catch her off Digit's back. Approaching Jackie quietly, I took hold of the reins and swung myself back in the saddle. It was a relief to be joining the others after the hour's delay.

The countryside continued to get steeper, and burnt tree stumps lined the rugged hillsides from fires that had swept through years earlier. By the time we'd slid to the bottom, we were relieved to have rolling terrain for the rest of the ride, making our way along river flats as we followed the map back to our starting point. At a ford in the river we

Top
Riding the Mustangs out in a 3000-acre paddock in search of cattle at NZ Ranch.

Bottom
Amanda cantering Deacon through a field of wild irises.

crossed over. The mares picked their way through eagerly, but the geldings paused on the river's edge, refusing to cross. After some gentle coaxing, Deacon bravely leapt across, but Gunnar refused to try, stubbornly backing away even though he'd crossed a number of rivers on our ride at Wilson's Creek; it took a good 10 minutes before he would ford the river. It wasn't surprising, given that the two geldings hadn't had much exposure to water, but the mares loved it — every time we passed a pond, they would divert from the path and gleefully throw themselves in the water. Happy to let them enjoy themselves, we loosened the reins and let them splash — although when Coyote showed signs of wanting to roll, Alexa had to make her leave quickly, before she, and the saddle, were drenched in muddy water.

THE FOLLOWING DAY, ON LIZ AND BOB'S recommendation, we woke at sunrise, loaded the horses and headed off to ride in the Eagle Cap Wilderness. Apparently the scenery was not to be missed, but after three hours of driving we were truly questioning whether it was going to be worth it. As we neared our destination, however, there was no doubting that the ride would be scenic. It was 7 miles (12 kilometres) each way to the Lookingglass Lake, and we were anticipating it taking a few hours, so had brought saddle packs and filled them with water, snacks and feed for the horses, then strapped them onto Coyote and Gunnar. Coyote might have seemed a strange choice, since she was still unpredictable to ride at times and the packs would bounce around on the horses' backs, but we felt sure she'd actually cope well as she was used to carrying things. Just to be sure, Kirsty led Coyote off Digit, getting her trotting and cantering to make sure she was used to the jostling, before Alexa mounted.

About 100 metres down the track we came across a log near the path, and although jumping in a Western saddle left a lot to be desired, we aimed for it. Most of the horses jumped it smoothly, but Coyote got a fright from the saddle packs on landing and took off along the trail. Regaining her balance, Alexa pulled her to a halt, patted her neck in reassurance and waited for the rest of us to catch up. The next hour was

Top
Jackie and I crossing a river in the Eagle Cap Wilderness.

Bottom
Amanda and Deacon jumping over a fallen log on our ride to Lookingglass Lake.

uneventful, and we gradually rose in altitude. The narrow dirt tracks, scattered with boulders and steps, made it impossible to go faster than a walk, and, on the odd occasion that we passed through a meadow, we would leave the path to trot and canter through the grass.

It was a spectacular landscape, with wild flowers, raging rivers and waterfalls cutting down between the two mountains we were riding between. At times the track followed flooded springs and small creeks, but it wasn't until we forded the main river that the two geldings were put through their biggest test. It was a fast-flowing river, and bravely Kirsty and I crossed first. Shoulder-deep Digit and Jackie ploughed through, eager to get to the dry ground on the other side; as we battled against the strong current the horses were pushed slightly downstream. When we finally made it across, we turned to watch Coyote lead the two geldings across. As the water grew deeper, they tensed. Although Gunnar kept his cool, Deacon lurched forward in fright when the water surged around his chest. It took all of Amanda's efforts to keep the gelding on his feet as he panicked in the deep water, and they rushed to shore, water flying as he leapt out of the river. She was lucky enough to stay dry; riding for the next few hours dripping wet wouldn't have been fun.

We continued following the main trail, although at times we were convinced we'd ridden too far. We rode through marsh-lands, jumped more logs and crossed laced rivers. At one point we had to ride through a shallow pool at the base of a cascading waterfall; the pool was no more than 5 metres in diameter and dropped off a steep cliff into another waterfall. The path was too narrow at this point to turn around in. We considered dismounting and leading the horses through, but Vicki was sure we could keep the horses steady, and ourselves dry, by riding through it. Again the mares led the way, and although water rained down on us from the incoming waterfall the horses kept going straight. Once I glanced over at the drop only metres away and was filled with dread; tightening my inside rein, I was careful to keep Jackie as close to the upper waterfall as I could. All five horses crossed safely; in fact, they were so unfazed that there was never a moment when we felt in danger. The path soon opened out into a forest, and as we weaved between the trees

Top
Coyote and Alexa
crossing a waterfall.

Middle and Bottom
Riding above the
snow line in the Eagle
Cap Wilderness.

we came across pockets of snow. As we climbed higher the snow grew deeper, and soon the path was obscured. Many times we back-tracked or rode in circles trying to find a way back on to the hidden path; the snow was making it difficult to navigate.

We'd been riding for almost three hours now, and sure that we must be almost at the lake we struggled on until finally the snow was behind us, and ahead steep switchbacks were evident around the side of the mountain. For the next 40 minutes we rode in single file along a treacherous path, occasionally dismounting to test out patches of snow and ice from where waterfalls had frozen over the track. The first two were passable, but the third one we reached was too long, too narrow and too icy to cross safely. Disappointed, we gave up — we'd ridden for almost four hours in search of the lake, only to have to turn around so close to the top.

With no other option we had to turn for home, but it couldn't have happened at a worst part of the trail. Turning the horses around would be hazardous, and one by one we climbed onto the rocks above the track so that they would have the full 3 feet (90 centimetres) of ledge for making the turn. Despite this Deacon lost his footing, his back legs hanging precariously off the edge — Amanda threw herself backwards, using her entire body weight and strength to pull him back onto the path. The rest of us struggled to keep our own horses steady while the young sorrel panicked, but the track was too narrow for us to go to their aid. We just watched in horror as Amanda battled gravity to keep Deacon upright. Finally, exhausted and shaking but safe, he stood facing back down the mountain, all four legs beneath him. For the next hour, as we retraced our route to the valley below, we paused every few minutes to rest Deacon, whose legs were still wobbling with exhaustion.

Finally, the worst was behind us and the track opened back out to grassy plains. Although it was getting late and storm clouds were gathering overhead, we stopped and unsaddled the horses so that they could graze and rest. It had been a gruelling climb up the mountain for us, too, and we collapsed on the ground, loosely holding our Mustangs' reins as they grazed on the fresh grass around us. All too soon it was time

Vicki carrying the injured baby elk off the mountain on Gunnar, who was just a week out of the BLM yards and only on his fifth ride.

to saddle up again; hugely tired, but trusting the horses to get us safely home, we gave our Mustangs their heads and let them carry us back the way we had come.

As we navigated a washed-out section of track, Gunnar, who was in the lead, paused and sidestepped towards the scrub. Looking in the direction he was avoiding, Vicki found a newborn elk lying on the side of the track, bones jutting from its sides. As she swung from the saddle and approached, it made no move to flee — too weak to do more than raise its head and look dully at her. Although no injuries were evident, it was obviously too young and weak to survive alone. We gave it a little water as it was clearly dehydrated.

Compelled to help it, Vicki lifted the elk in her arms and showed it to Gunnar, then passed it to Amanda while she mounted. Alexa stood in front of the palomino to reassure him while Amanda passed the baby elk up into Vicki's arms. The horse, although uncertain, stood steadily. Vicki placed the elk over the saddle, with its legs hanging on either side of the horse's shoulders, then turned Gunnar and we made our way down the track. Although Gunnar was startled several times by the elk starting to slip off and crying in distress, Vicki finally got them both settled, using a spare jacket to blindfold the elk to keep it calm.

Over the next two hours, Gunnar became well used to the occasional movement and noise coming from the baby animal and remained steady. After a while, the blindfold was taken off and it would twist its head around Vicki's side to watch us riding behind; it was curious by nature and had sparked up a lot since we'd given it the water. Seven hours after we'd left the car park, we crossed the final bridge and arrived back at the head of the trail. Grabbing the map — which we had left behind — we quickly spotted that we'd missed a turn-off. The lake we had almost reached at the top of the mountain was Glacier Lake, not Lookingglass Lake, which was significantly closer and appeared to be on much flatter terrain!

Totally exhausted, we loaded the horses and drove the seemingly endless three hours back to NZ Ranch, stumbling to the back of the trailer to let the horses out and settle them into the barn for the night.

Liz quickly found some formula for the elk — it was helpful that we were staying with a vet who was experienced in rehabilitating wildlife, and we had no doubt it would be in good hands.

After a quick meal, we settled into the spa and shared our adventures from the day. Liz then told us a story about two horses she'd treated years earlier. Two cowboys had trailered their horses to the vet clinic, both animals looked like they'd been hit by a truck although they had no major injuries or breaks. Not believing the cowboys' story about a paddock accident, she pried the truth from them. They'd taken two horses up a narrow track and been hit by an avalanche of rocks. Both horses toppled off the ledge, one falling down the sheer rocky face, flipping over until it reached the bottom and lay still in a pile of rocks. The other horse was trapped on a second ledge halfway down the cliff. Although it had struggled to its feet and was standing, there was no chance it making it off the ledge alive; in the remote location a rescue mission was virtually impossible. Not wanting the horse to starve to death, or panic and fall like the first horse, the cowboy lined it up in the sights of his gun and pulled the trigger. The shot hit its mark and the horse toppled off the ledge to join the first horse at the bottom. Distraught, the two guys hiked off the mountain, camped overnight in their truck and hiked back up the canyon the next morning to retrieve their gear and supplies from the horses' saddle packs.

As they made their way between the towering walls of cliff, they froze — sure that they were seeing ghosts. Ahead of them, looking a little the worse for wear but alive, were their two horses, who pricked up their ears eagerly when they saw their human companions. As soon as they got the horses back to the trailer the cowboys sped to the vet clinic for Liz to treat them.

Relieved that Deacon's story hadn't had a similarly dramatic ending, we sighed and sank deeper into the bubbling water, letting the warmth ease the aches after our long day in the saddle.

The Palomino Valley BLM yards in Nevada, a long-term holding facility which yards 1800 wild horses.

CHAPTER 9

All the wild horses

By sunrise we were on the road again, and things were about to get interesting. We were staying one night with Jen, the equine dentist we'd met a couple of days earlier, and then we were into the unknown with no plans in place — neither for where we were going or where we would spend our nights. Our only goal was to make it to the Grand Canyon before heading back for the competition. But first we had to return to Matt and Stacie's — to collect Red and Spring; having had no luck finding a wild horse sanctuary for them, we were forced to return them to the BLM yards at Boise.

Although inevitable, it was devastating. The two mares had come to us wild, and as we led them back through the BLM yards we felt that we were betraying much of the trust they'd placed in us. They'd driven over a thousand miles with us, allowed us to touch, catch and ride them and pick up their feet. We'd led them through snowstorms, let them splash and roll in mountain rivers, and set them free in pastures to gallop and graze . . . and now, after this taste of freedom, they were back in the yards, once again inmates with a life sentence. The vet reports almost guaranteed that the mares would never leave these yards; with 50,000 Mustangs to choose from, it would make no sense for someone to re-home a horse that already had soundness issues. There was also a chance that Spring, with her hopeless vet report, would be euthanised. Although this was heartbreaking to hear, because the mare was so sweet, we really had no choice in the matter — the horses were BLM property. Re-entering the yard, Amanda gave Spring one last hug, and with tears in her eyes she smiled bravely and whispered goodbye. It was a sombre drive back to the ranch. As soon as we arrived, we caught and loaded our other horses before saying our farewells to Matt and Stacie. We wouldn't be seeing them again until the Extreme Mustang Makeover in two months' time, and it would be interesting to see how their horses would progress; so far neither had been ridden.

It was already late evening by the time we arrived at Jen's, and we enjoyed catching up with her again. Dan, the vet who'd sedated the horses for their teeth to be done, came around for dinner, and we had an evening of good food and great company. The next morning Jen took us to Black Canyon Dam to swim the horses, joining us with her own thoroughbred. For over an hour we played in the water: swimming in the deeper current, letting the horses roll in the shallows, and laughing hysterically as we attempted to stand on the horses' backs while they waded though the deep water. We'd planned to head to Reno, in Nevada, that evening, but by the time we were ready it was late afternoon and we had seven hours of driving ahead of us, so Jen suggested we stay with one of her clients halfway. Leaving her to make arrangements, we began our long drive south. We were relieved to get the call to say they were expecting us, and we arrived just after sunset, settling the horses into the yards by nightfall. It must have been inconvenient to have a truck full of complete strangers arrive on the doorstep at 9 p.m., but they couldn't have been more gracious — offering us food, showers, beds to sleep in (although we'd insisted the trailer was fine) and hay for the horses.

By sunrise we were back on the road, and by midday we finally neared Reno. Our first stop was the Palomino Valley National Wild Horse and Burro Facility; unlike Boise with just 100 horses, it was a long-term holding facility with close to 1800. The largest such facility in America, it was used for sorting most of the wild Mustangs captured, as the state of Nevada contained 50 per cent of the nation's wild horse population. We were keen to add another Mustang to our collection — a spare would be invaluable as a pack horse, and if one were to go lame we would still have enough horses to ride out on together. Just before we got there we passed a huge equestrian venue, and on the off-chance they had yards available we called in and asked. It was US$20 per horse per night, and we spent some time deliberating — we were planning to be in Reno for two nights, staying with an aunty we'd never met, and US$200, or NZ$300, spent on basic yards for the horses seemed steep. The practicality of it won us over, though — not only was it close to Palomino Valley, but the price also included the use of the indoor arena, which was set up with a hunter-jumper course. We would be able to school the horses around the jumps, an experience that would be hugely beneficial — teaching them not only to jump but also to work in an indoor venue similar to where the competition would be held.

After settling the horses into the stables, we headed to the BLM yards and introduced ourselves. Like the team at Boise, they were good guys who were looking out for the horses' best interests. Although there were almost 2000 horses, they could tell us about many on sight, and were also proactive in raising awareness about the plight of the Mustangs, frequently visiting schools and doing demos to increase public adoption rates.

Although we hadn't made an appointment, they offered to show us around the horses in their truck. Most of the large corrals contained between 100 and 300 horses, split into groups by age and gender, and as we drove through, the more curious ones mobbed the truck, used to seeing it delivering hay. Even in captivity the herd dynamics were strong, the horses obviously having formed bonds with others, and it was interesting to see how they grouped themselves. Many horses stood out in just the first yard, although there were hundreds of horses in the pen. Amanda was impressed by a large chestnut gelding, about six years old; although obviously bigger than the others, it was impossible to gauge how tall he was. Vicki and Amanda were quite keen for our sixth Mustang to be hack height (at least 15.3 hands), because if it showed talent they were hoping to train it for themselves as a potential showjumper. The BLM guy estimated the chestnut at 15.2 hands, which wasn't quite tall enough — anything between 15.3 and 16.2 hands would be ideal, although we knew that the bigger horses, much like our Kaimanawas in New Zealand, were rare. The average height for a Mustang seemed to be 14 to 15 hands and the BLM guy agreed, although he took great pleasure in showing us a 17-hand gelding in the next yard.

This lanky giant, although huge, didn't have the correct conformation for jumping, and we moved on. The third pen was slightly smaller, and the horses had unsightly numbers branded across their rumps as well as the traditional Mustang brand on their necks. These were the horse deemed unsuitable to re-home by the BLM — those over seven or with three strikes. Either a lack of available homes in their younger years or being captured in their later years meant that these horses were now sentenced to a lifetime in the yards. Beyond curious, we asked plenty of

Top
Many of the horses in the BLM yards are curious about people — some because they know no other life, having been born in the yards, and others from boredom or constant exposure to humans bringing them feed.

Middle
Each yard at Palomino Valley contains up to 300 horses, sorted by age and gender.

Bottom
Mustangs over the age of seven years, or those that are three-strike horses, are branded on their rumps and deemed unsuitable to re-home.

questions and soon had an insight into why the government had decided that seven years old was the cut-off point. To us, after working with older Kaimanawa mares and stallions straight from the wild — some as old as 18 — it seemed unlikely that these horses, accustomed to yards and people after years of being in captivity, would be impossible to train; in fact, we could have guaranteed it. But the BLM had a point: why re-home the older ones when there were thousands upon thousands of younger, easier and probably healthier horses available to adopt? Why make the taming process that much harder when there were so few homes available? Each year, the re-homing numbers were so low that they weren't even keeping up with the number of horses being mustered and the 50,000 currently in captivity was increasing rapidly. Hundreds of captive Mustangs across America were turning seven every year and being branded as lost causes because of a dire lack of interest. We had no doubt that these horses, which continued to impress us at every turn, were one of America's greatest assets being wasted. So many people were breeding horses all over the country, investing time and money into producing offspring — many of which would be less suited to their needs than something they could re-home from the BLM yards.

As we watched the older horses, many of which had at least 20 years of life ahead of them, it seemed criminal that they would spend all of that time in these yards, wandering around in boredom while waiting for hay to come, desensitised to the flies biting them in summer and shaking from a lack of shelter in the worst winter snowstorms. They had no grass to eat, no hope of galloping across plains and — because of the brand on their rumps — little to no chance of being offered a second chance at freedom. Curious, the horses watched us, creeping closer; Amanda and Kirsty, who had been standing off to the side, were soon surrounded. Many of these wild horses were probably the ones most used to humans; for they had spent the majority of their lives in confinement, year after year after year becoming familiar with the humans that visited them twice a day with their feed.

In the next pen were 100 freshly mustered horses from Fish Creek, still in poor condition and looking stunted from malnutrition. They'd arrived during a summer drought six months earlier, and even after good feeding the ribs of many were still visible. These horses were watchful, wary and wild, wheeling around the yard, snorting and stirring up dust, as we stood at the fence watching them. Humans were still something they feared; they were the most like the Kaimanawas we train in New Zealand, as opposed to those Mustangs that have had time to acclimatise to captivity.

The final yard we saw was filled with 300 geldings aged three to four years. We stood at the fences, picking long grass for them, and about 50 became curious and wandered over. We leant over the rails for half an hour while the horses milled around below us, some stretching their necks up to lip the grass from our outstretched hands and letting us touch them. This pen offered the nicest quality so far: the size, colour and confirmation of these horses were outstanding. We could have easily walked away with 100 of them.

After much discussion, re-checking each horse's conformation and watching them move around the yards, we narrowed our favourites down to three — the big chestnut from the first yard and two roan (a horse of mainly one colour, with white hairs mixed in) geldings from the last mob. We pointed them out to the BLM staff, but it then became apparent that these horses couldn't join us; unlike Boise, the horses at Palomino Valley needed to have vet work, foot trimming and blood tests done before they were allowed to be transported, especially across state lines. Since we were due in Salt Lake City — a nine-hour drive to the east — in just two days' time for an interview for New Zealand television, it wasn't possible. The staff suggested we look at Mustangs in Delta, Utah, instead — another short-term facility that would have all the health papers up-to-date.

RETURNING TO THE EQUESTRIAN FACILITY WE SADDLED our horses, using our English jumping saddles for the first time in weeks. First we took the three mares into the indoor arena, setting the jumps low to get them used to the poles. It was the horses' first real schooling session; the first time they'd been ridden in a bit or worked in a circle.

TOP
Coyote objected strongly to being given direction and even by day 50, halfway
through our training, she was unpredictable if asked to do something new.

BOTTOM
Amanda teaching Deacon how to jump over poles for the first time, at an indoor arena in Reno.

All three were confused at times, but gradually Jackie and Digit relaxed, softened and started producing lovely work. Coyote, however, resorted to her more disreputable self: rearing, leaping and broncoing every time she had to leave her friends. Unlike the other two she was still being ridden in a halter as she opposed the idea of a bit, and would gnaw on it and become angry and agitated. Ignoring Coyote's antics, Alexa remained steady in the saddle and gradually worked her out of it, producing consistency in pace and correct direction. Thoroughly warmed up, we then approached a small crossbar, jumping it a few times until the horses understood what was being asked of them. From there we progressed to small oxers and uprights, and then walls and fillers. The jumps were low enough that the horses could jump them from a standstill if they hesitated; once they were confident, we increased the height before cantering around the course again.

By the end of their first session the mares were cantering around jumps up to 90 centimetres and showing good form. The jumps were a natural step up from the logs on the trails, and we were impressed by how quickly they got the hang of it. Next out were Gunnar and Deacon, and although they'd been ridden fewer than 10 times and were only two weeks out of the BLM yards, they were as good as the mares. They, too, progressed up the heights until they were cantering into decent oxers; in fact, they showed even more talent than the mares. Deacon was probably the most impressive, and with maturity we had no doubt that he'd develop into a top-level hunter-jumper. The next day we repeated the lessons, and by the end of it all five Mustangs were jumping up to 1 metre. It would have to be a priority to find jumps along our way, because the mares were certainly talented enough to jump in the freestyle element of their routines.

We'd vaguely heard about a wild horse programme in a nearby prison and were keen to know more. After a bit of research, we found the contact for Northern Nevada Correctional Center in Carson City, about 30 minutes out of Reno. To our surprise, the inmates were showcasing their trained Mustangs at a public auction the following day, with over 20 saddle-trained horses available for adoption. Stoked about the timing, we decided to visit, interested to see how far advanced the Mustangs would be after the 90 days of training they were given, and to witness first-hand the impact it was having on the lives of the men entrusted with taming them.

THE NEXT MORNING, WE ROSE EARLY TO take the horses to Carson City, needing to find an equine property nearby to yard our horses at while we attended the auction. Having the horses nearby would save us some serious back-tracking, and time was tight. We arrived at the prison early and were surprised by the ready access we had to the prisoners. Starting at one end we walked along the fence line, asking the inmates about their Mustangs, how the training programme had changed their lives, and how much experience they had with horses. They were open about their crimes, which varied from first-time offences through assault-and-battery to careers in crime with most of the offender's life spent behind bars. They were, however, unanimous about how much working with the Mustangs was changing their lives. The horses were teaching them patience and empathy for others, while also giving them hope for a better future. For many of these men, the skills they were learning while taming and training the horses would be invaluable in terms of a career option when they walked out of prison in one, two, or in some cases, 20 years.

The horses they'd trained also varied. The smallest was just 13.2 hands; and a Kiger dun from Oregon, with black stripes on its legs, stood out at 15.3 hands. Not only was it big, but it had something special about it and looked like it was built for jumping. We chatted with Bragg, his trainer, for a bit and he told us about the horse's strengths and weaknesses. Bragg was one of the most experienced trainers in the Wild Horse Inmate Program and had been training two horses for the auction. Pointing out his other horse, a bay hitched to the fence, he explained that this one had a few issues and he wasn't sure if anyone would adopt it; it was a little unpredictable, could buck, and had mouthing issues so was happier when ridden bitless.

Watching the gelding we could understand Bragg's concerns — even

Jackie (top) and Digit's (bottom) first time jumping over poles, although they had previously jumped over logs and barrels on our travels.

Top
One of the inmates loading Sleepy Brown onto our trailer, who we later nicknamed Bragg.

Bottom
Smith, Bragg and Parker, our three prison Mustangs who were trained as part of the
Wild Horses Inmate Program at the Northern Nevada Correctional Center.

tied up, with no rider on, he was prancing and throwing himself sideways, twisting and bucking on the spot. Bragg admitted that the horse's issues could possibly have been enhanced by a clash in personalities — the highly reactive gelding was overly sensitive and the inmate had self-confessed anger issues, something he'd had to confront and work on over the past 90 days of taming the bay gelding. Since he'd had two horses to train, he'd had just three hours a day with each; the other horses had had up to six hours of contact time with their assigned inmates. We glanced at each other in surprise; never in our lives had we worked a horse that intensively. Calling them 90-day horses was hugely under-representing the amount of training they'd undergone, between two and six times what a normal trainer would provide.

Moving on, we chatted to a man named Smith about the palomino he was riding, and were intrigued to learn that he'd never sat on a horse before joining the programme three months earlier. When we asked how that had gone for him, he admitted that the first time he'd tried to ride the Mustang he'd been bucked off and knocked out, but since then he'd managed to stay on. He told us that working with the horse had helped him realise the value of relationships, and that he'd since reconnected with his daughter. After spending more than a decade in prison, he wished he'd been accepted into the wild horse programme earlier, because being out in the sun and doing physical work was changing his life; it was giving him a reason to get up in the morning, and for the first time he cared about the future — something that had slipped away over the years he'd spent locked up in a cell.

As the announcer called for everyone to take their seats, we moved over to the grandstands overlooking the arena; Vicki disappeared into the crowd. After a quick introduction, all of the Mustangs entered the arena in a drill, showcasing team-work and an impressive level of training. The three most advanced horses, including the Kiger dun that we had fancied, were showcased well, carrying flags in the lead. They would undoubtedly attract some of the highest prices at auction. Vicki joined us halfway through, a cheeky grin on her face and waving a bidding number at us; although we had said that we wouldn't take any Mustangs home with us, Vicki was clearly considering bidding.

Still in formation the Mustangs left the arena, and immediately the first horse returned to be auctioned. One after one they were put through their paces: walking, trotting and cantering around the arena before the rider dismounted and picked up all four feet. Bidding then began. Prices ranged from US$200 to US$2700, the Kiger dun being the highest-priced horse midway through the auction. Then a chestnut gelding entered the ring and the announcer, rather than praising the horse and singing his accolades like he'd done with the others, warned people to bid wisely. This was the most difficult horse available; he had a bad reputation for bucking riders off, especially when first ridden (known as being cold-backed). It wasn't the horse's fault — he'd been trained by a hot-headed inmate who was new to the programme and had been given a rough beginning to domestication. This inmate was no longer a part of the programme, and an experienced guy had stepped in for the past three weeks in the hope of training the horse sufficiently to find him a home. The crowd went quiet, not prepared to bid on a such an unpromising horse; indeed, as we watched him work he was obviously giving his trainer a rough ride. The auctioneer commented that most of the horses that passed in below the reserve of US$150 were returned to the BLM yards as one-strike horses, diminishing their chances of being re-homed.

The call went up for the last chance to bid, and to my surprise the auctioneer raised his hand, acknowledging a bid for $150. Dead silence followed, and as it was obvious that no one else would bid, he did the final calling, pointed in our direction and said 'Sold, to the young lady in the front row.' We all gaped at a sheepish Amanda; a difficult Mustang with a bad reputation was the last thing we needed on our journey. I put my head in my hands, laughing quietly to myself — it was such an Amanda thing to do and I shouldn't have been surprised.

A few more horses were presented, and sold for ridiculously low prices. When the beautiful palomino entered the ring, I sat up; although he was green, we expected him to sell for top dollar with his striking colour, his size and relaxed temperament. When the bidding stalled at $500, I was shocked that such a lovely horse would sell so cheaply; grabbing Vicki's bidding number I raised it in the air, hoping to push other buyers to increase their bids. The plan backfired — silence followed, and it seemed that I had accidently bought a horse. Even worse, it had cost me over three times as much as Amanda's new addition. Laughing, Vicki pushed me off my seat, telling me I had better go and meet the latest horse in my life, and I slinked over to the corral fence to chat with Smith and reacquaint myself with the palomino.

Amanda soon bounded over with a guilty grin. I looked at her sharply — when I'd left, there had only been one more horse to auction off; surely she hadn't bought another one? But sure enough she had, buying the difficult bay gelding for just $150; again the only bidder. Joining me at the rails she waited for Bragg to ride over on the Mustang. When I saw the man's face, I couldn't fault Amanda's decision. His relief was hugely evident on his face as he thanked Amanda for giving his horse a chance. He'd been so worried that after all the love and time he'd put into the horse it would have to return to the BLM yards; he couldn't be happier that the bay was going to a good home, and talked Amanda through everything to watch out for.

The auction had taken much longer than anticipated, and filling out the paperwork took even more time. By the time we were done it was mid-afternoon; even if everything went smoothly we wouldn't be arriving at Salt Lake City until the early hours of the morning. The three new horses loaded well, and we said our final goodbyes to the inmates, promising to keep them updated on the horses' progress. After squeezing our other five Mustangs on the trailer, too, with a full load we began our long drive to Utah.

Riding our Mustangs on
Antelope Island overlooking
the Great Salt Lakes, Utah.

CHAPTER 10

Heading into Utah

Hour after hour we drove, and with Vicki the only one confident driving with such a heavy load or experienced pulling a trailer, it was especially tiring for her. To keep her awake, we talked about life in general and plans for the future; it was inspiring and productive. Some of our best brainstorming sessions are done in trucks, as these are some of the few times we are all together uninterrupted.

Despite us talking to keep her awake, Vicki was lagging; it was the early hours of the morning and she'd been driving with minimal rest for over seven hours. We had underestimated the distance to our final destination, and too tired to continue we kept an eye out for somewhere to stop. An hour later we finally drove into West Wendover; like many of the small towns we'd driven through in Nevada, it seemed to exist solely for gambling. After driving past countless casinos, we stumbled across the rodeo grounds. By the time we'd settled our horses into the yards, with hay and water, it was four o'clock in the morning; exhausted, we checked into a hotel. We still had three hours of driving ahead of us and had to be at Antelope Island to meet the film crew by 10 a.m., so we'd be lucky to get two hours of sleep. The only reason we didn't sleep in the truck was because we were all in desperate need of showers and had to be looking half-decent for filming. Our TV series *Keeping Up With the Kaimanawas* was airing in New Zealand in two days' time, and a film crew had flown over from New York to film us riding the Mustangs for an interest piece to screen on *One News* the same night.

We'd chosen Antelope Island because we had heard you could ride among buffalo, and it looked stunning in photos, overlooking the Great Salt Lakes. What we *hadn't* planned for were the bugs — the mosquitos were giant in comparison to what we were used to at home, and were relentless. By the time we had the horses saddled, all of us — cameraman, ourselves and the horses — were bleeding; even insect-repellent was ineffective. Desperate to get this over as fast as possible, we cantered Jackie, Deacon and Gunnar over the ridge-line and pushed our way through reeds that towered above our horses before riding down to the salt lakes for scenic shots. Walking was impossible because the bugs clung to us, biting us through our clothes and also agitating the horses;

to escape the swarms that followed us, we urged the Mustangs forward into a gallop, eventually halting beside the cameraman whose legs were dripping with blood from the savage bites.

We held the horses for a quick interview, then immediately loaded them onto the trailer and hightailed it out of there. All our grand plans of riding the trails rounding up buffalo were forgotten in our desperate attempt to flee, and we were now at a loss as to what to do. Our first priority was finding somewhere to keep the horses — Jen, our equine dentist, couldn't get down for a couple of days, and the prison geldings urgently needed their teeth done; two of them had wolf teeth and retained caps, which could explain much of the contact issues the inmates had been having. There were no rodeo or showgrounds available, and our only option seemed to be an equestrian venue with stalls at US$30 per horse per night. With eight Mustangs it was now going to cost us US$480 (almost NZ$700) for the two days, and unable to justify this level of expense we decided to knock on strangers' doors to see what we could find.

It took a while navigating side streets and country lanes before we found a property with fencing high enough to contain Mustangs. Nervous and unsure how successful we would be, Alexa and I introduced ourselves to the man who answered the door, explained our predicament and pointed out the yards alongside the house. The Mormon family was rushing out to church, and politely explained that although they owned the yards, they'd already leased them out to a farmer so couldn't help. Disappointed but not totally disheartened by the experience, we continued driving. A hundred metres down the road we passed a field with high fencing, and again stopped to ask.

The lady who opened the door looked past us, saw the horse trailer, waved for us to follow her and said she'd show us where the gates were. Since we hadn't even spoken yet, we stood there in confusion, unsure how she knew we were looking for a place to keep our horses. After a few minutes, we realised that she must have been expecting someone else to arrive with horses to graze her pasture, so explained that while we were looking for a pasture for our Mustangs, we weren't the people she was expecting. Looking briefly confused, the lovely lady listened to our story and then dashed inside to call the other people and delay their arrival for a few days so that she could offer us the use of her field during our stay in Salt Lake City.

Amazed and slightly dazed at the bizarre turn of events, we unloaded the horses. There was only one large field, so we set them all free together. It was the prison Mustangs' first time on grass since they'd been mustered from the wild, and we just hoped they'd let us catch them again. Once they were settled, we went off in search of a hotel room — this time tomorrow we'd be on TV, which seemed very odd, and we thought we'd better have access to power and internet so we could watch at least some of the episodes before they screened. As soon as we had checked in, we crawled into bed; we were all too shattered to do anything after so little sleep the night before, and were quite happy to sleep both the afternoon and the night away.

The next morning, we woke refreshed and headed down to the field to work the horses. First up was Parker, the cold-backed and difficult chestnut. He was friendly and easy to catch, and stood to be saddled. Since his teeth hadn't been done yet, Vicki used a bosal, and after lungeing him for a few minutes she quietly mounted. Prepared for the worst but hoping for the best, she sat quietly and then gently asked him to walk. We'd been warned that the first steps forward were when he was most likely to explode, but he looked bored and relaxed as they walked in a circle. Asking him forward again, they trotted, and then cantered, around the field for 20 minutes. Our first US$150 Mustang hadn't put a foot wrong; pleased, Vicki unsaddled him and let him loose to graze. Next up was Smith, the palomino, whom Vicki rode while Bragg stood to be saddled for Amanda to mount. We'd expected Smith to be quiet, and sure enough he was, although he didn't have the best mouth and was noticeably green, unable to maintain straight lines or a canter for long. It was evident that he'd been trained by someone unused to horses, but the fundamentals were there — he was steady and quiet and would make a valuable addition to our team. Bragg, the other 'problem horse', also surprised us; although he appeared distracted at times and Amanda

Top
Amanda's first ride on Bragg, two days after we bought him at the prison auction.

Bottom
Vicki's first ride on Parker was uneventful.

said that if he was a kid he'd probably have ADHD, in general he was kind and willing. Relieved, we congratulated each other on our latest additions. Now that we were road-tripping in earnest, we needed horses that could already be caught and saddled — far easier than a Mustang fresh out of the BLM yards.

When her time came, Coyote was the worst she'd ever been. She'd had a soft snaffle-bit on a few times, and although she didn't enjoy it she had become accustomed to it. Feeling that she was ready to be mouthed, Alexa put the gear on her. However, when she asked the mare to go out on the circle on a lunge line and work forward into the contact provided by the bit, Coyote exploded, rearing and striking out in defiance and hitting Alexa. With tears streaming down her face — more from frustration and confusion than pain — Alexa asked the mare to go out on the circle again. Coyote just didn't like change or being told what to do, and it took a long time for the resentful mare to settle down and soften her attitude. Alexa had been patient and gentle with Coyote from the beginning, but anything new, no matter how simple, was a huge battle, and she had real doubts that the mare would be ready for re-homing in just nine weeks. It was both disheartening and worrying.

That night Jen arrived, and with six of us in the room it was a tight squeeze. We watched the first episode of *Keeping Up With the Kaimanawas* to see what people at home would be viewing in just a couple of hours' time. The editor and director had done a great job — although it was obviously 'reality TV' and they had maximised on the drama, it wasn't totally cringe-making. It showed both the highs and the lows of taming wild horses, and — more importantly — the passion and time needed to make it successful. In quick succession we watched the next seven episodes, too, and by the end of it were looking at each in relief. There were certainly parts that weren't really in context and parts that we wished hadn't been included, but we could live with that — it was real and honest and we hoped it would go down well. If the ratings were poor or the feedback too negative, I think we might have relocated to America for good.

We woke the next morning to hundreds of emails, messages and comments about the premiere and were relieved to hear how well it had been taken; people seemed excited to watch the second episode. Looking around at the mess we were living in, we couldn't help but laugh — there was nothing glamorous about the way we were travelling, and if people could see us now it would shatter any misconceptions about television personalities. We were certainly not your normal 'reality stars' and weren't afraid to rough it.

The next morning we rode the prison Mustangs bareback and in halters, and again they were easy; we'd certainly got value for money on these horses and couldn't understand their being difficult — so far they hadn't put a hoof wrong. Jen and the vet soon got to work on their teeth, and with their dental issues taken care of we were looking forward to these horses being accepting of a bit. Since having eight horses on the road was totally impractical, Jen had agreed to take Gunnar and Deacon back to her place to graze until we could loop back and collect them. At three and four years old, they'd already learnt so much and a rest would do them good — unlike the rest of the horses, neither was fit enough to tackle the trails we planned to ride through in Utah, Arizona and Colorado.

With the horses' teeth done, Vicki shod Parker, Smith and Bragg so that they would be ready for some big rides. We then said goodbye to Dori, who owned the field, and her neighbours Jay and Susan, who had become good friends. Jay had popped over every day to watch us work with the horses and was fascinated by our journey. As a farewell, he gave us beautiful wood carvings he'd created by hand. Amanda's was a football with jade inlays replicating the stitching; it was worth thousands of dollars and Amanda tried to return it, knowing just how valuable it was, but Jay was adamant that she keep it. Thanking him profusely, she told him she'd value it forever and that it would serve as a reminder of their generosity, friendship and our time in America.

FROM SALT LAKE CITY WE HEADED SOUTH towards the Delta BLM yards. The 800 horses kept there included many of the Kiger Mustangs, which were said to have the purest Spanish blood and were different from the other Mustangs. On our way we stopped at Utah Lake to swim the horses. It was fairly average — mushy underfoot and the water smelt stale — but the mares were dynamos in the water. The prison geldings were unsure and hesitant; as they'd had 90 days of training, as opposed to our mares' 50 days, it was sometimes easy to forget how little life experience they'd had until now.

Three hours later we drove through Delta; it was a 'blink and you'll miss it' kind of place, and it wasn't until we reached the outskirts of the town that we realised that we'd already driven through it and so back-tracked to find suitable yards for the horses. A local guy playing baseball with his family in a nearby reserve directed us to the showgrounds, telling us to help ourselves to the yards, and soon we were settling our horses in. Our next stop was the BLM yards which were again managed by a proactive guy who was excited to share stories about the Mustangs and show us the horses available. As we walked from yard to yard it was impossible not to notice how fat some of them were. Apparently, because of welfare groups and animal rights activists they had to be very careful that they didn't have horses in poor condition; because of this they had to feed to the lowest dominator in each yard, meaning that many were overweight. Not having much room to move around didn't help, and as the yards were understaffed many horses' hooves were also overdue for trimming.

The Kiger and Sulphur horses, known for their colouring and Spanish descent, were easily distinguishable from the rest and had a reputation for being more difficult to tame. While some were stunning types, others had unusual conformation and weren't ones we would re-home by choice. We now had our three EMM and three prison Mustangs but only five riders, so unless we led one out on every ride there would always be one horse left behind. It would be better to have another horse to keep it company, so we decided to re-home one from these yards; the last Mustang to join our growing team. Eventually we narrowed it down to two horses in the pen of older mares. Both had been re-homed previously but had been returned to the BLM yards within days, so they were just US$25.

Top
Kiger Mustangs at the BLM yards in Utah.

Bottom
A sorrel Mustang, who was mustered from California, caught our eye from the 800 horses at the Utah yards. We re-homed her through the TIP program and named her Rayna.

Finally, we settled on the lighter chestnut. She was separated from the others and run into the yards to be processed. Her hooves were long overdue for a trim, and wanting to get it done gently and correctly we asked if we could do them ourselves after leaving. Agreeing, the staff put her into the squeeze crush to be haltered and the feisty red-head reared and threw herself against the walls in distress. It wasn't until the halter was on and she was released into a smaller yard that we noticed blood on the ground; she'd sliced a gash into her lower leg that would need urgent care. Luckily we had plenty of vet supplies in the trailer, and our first priority back at the showgrounds would be to get her handled enough to treat.

Over the next 10 minutes, Vicki spent time getting the mare used to the weight of the rope and responding to the halter. Once she had the basics sorted, Vicki led her forward to the base of the trailer, which we'd positioned at the end of the race. After hesitating for a few seconds, the mare bolted on board and we closed the door. The hard part behind us, we headed inside to finish off the paperwork and ask some questions; we were curious about the muster process, the BLM's involvement and how activists fitted into the scene. The manager was open to discussing it with us, perhaps because of our neutral position. We had been in America for just over nine weeks, soaking up as much knowledge about the wild horse problem as we could, and had read and watched plenty about the Mustangs beforehand. We were able to see both sides of the story, as opposed to the BLM and the activists who were tightly focused on their own agendas. From where we were sitting, both agendas had merit, and we listened with interest as the manager told us of legal battles instigated by activists that had endangered the welfare of wild Mustangs.

Once, during a drought in Nevada, the BLM had identified a starving herd with a very limited supply of water; experts had estimated that these horses had only months left before they exhausted the natural resources. To allow them to survive, and to ease pressure on the land, the BLM planned for a round-up eight weeks later, allowing just enough time to organise the logistics. But activists sued the government to prevent the round-up, tying things up in court for months. Meanwhile, the BLM

Rayna panicked during
the sorting process and
badly cut her leg.

dropped hay and water off to the horses daily, but the wild Mustangs were wary of the troughs and refused to drink from them. So, a tank of water was dropped off out of sight behind the hills and pipes were placed in the ground to fill a natural pond. However, all the wildlife in the area came to rely on the supplemented food and water, and the horses didn't always get enough. By the time the BLM had won the legal battle and the muster was able to take place, the horses were so weak that two died while being transported. The activists blamed the government for these deaths, but the BLM steadfastly believe that the horses wouldn't have died if the muster had been carried out earlier.

Of course this was only one side of the story, and it was impossible to form an opinion on who was right and who was wrong. But this, and other similar stories, certainly made us appreciate the good working relationship between the Department of Conservation, the New Zealand Army and Kaimanawa Heritage Horses — the three key players in the management of wild horses in our own country.

With our heads spinning from horrific tales about Mustanging — where men 'celebrate' their coming of age by roping a wild Mustang or Burro and slicing off an ear — and wild Mustangs being hobbled and left to die on the range, we made our way back to the truck, a little disheartened about humankind. To distract ourselves, we discussed potential names for our new Mustang, and decided on Rayna to stay with the Nashville theme we'd used for Deacon and Gunnar. As soon as we unloaded, Vicki set to work getting the mare accustomed to being touched and having her legs picked up. Soon her hooves were trimmed and her injured leg bandaged, and with darkness approaching we laid out our bedding for the night. We'd parked in an undercover lean-to off to the side of the Western arena, and rather than setting up the trailer we spread our mattresses over the concrete and slept out in the open.

THE NEXT MORNING DAWNED HOTTER THAN ANY we had experienced so far, and we saddled up early to get a ride in before the worst of the summer's heat. The arena was set up with barrels, and we worked our horses around them, before moving them together to make a jump for the mares — first laying them on their side, then (for Jackie and Digit) standing them upright to offer a higher obstacle.

By 9 a.m., it was too hot to move. Even reading in the shade was miserable — it never gets this hot in New Zealand and we weren't sure how to cope with the rising temperature. By midday we were desperate for something to relieve the heat, so we emptied out a water trough, scrubbed it clean and dragged it under the shelter before filling it with water. Stripping down to bikinis we all piled in and sat in the water for hours, enjoying the novelty of being cool. By early evening the sun had started to fade and we headed out to work with Rayna again. The six-year-old mare was progressing well, and was starting to get the concept of being led and being touched; she even stood calmly while Vicki lay across her back. With her injury it would be a few days before she could be ridden, but there was still plenty she could learn in the meantime.

The next day was much the same except that we went off in search of hay, coming back with 10 bales strapped to the front wall of the trailer; there was no space to carry it anywhere else. Dusty and hot from working in the midday heat, we hung a hose from the roof of the shelter as a makeshift shower. After cooling off in the water trough again, we took turns shampooing our hair under the hose. Alexa's shower was interrupted by two cowboys riding past to use the Western arena. Although wearing a bikini, she was mortified and quickly dived for a towel before scurrying back to the trailer to get dressed.

That night, after the horses had been worked, we practised loading with Rayna and again she walked straight on. We were planning to leave at first light and head south-west in search of wild Mustangs in the Sulphur Mountains. Following the slightly vague directions given to us by the BLM manager, we turned onto a gravel road and continued — sure enough, half an hour later we saw a herd of wild horses. Their colours were unusual: alongside a few common-coloured mares were a stunning red dun filly with distinctive Kiger stripes on her legs and a grullo stallion (grullos are black horses with the dun gene; they range in colour from light silvery white to dark chocolate brown, and some look almost black). The horses startled easily; rounding up his herd, the stallion moved them well off the road and they galloped away, stopping to watch us warily from a distance.

Hoping to find a more receptive herd we carried on, stopping when we found a lone grullo stallion galloping up and down a fence line that kept ranch cattle from grazing on public lands. Assuming that another herd was close by, we unloaded and saddled up while the stallion watched us with interest. Soon we were on our way, trotting over the rough terrain and weaving between the cacti and rocks scattered across the ground. Our instincts about the stallion had been right — as we crested a rise we came upon a large herd, which took flight. Our Mustangs were curious and settled into a canter to keep up with them, and, rather than fleeing, the wild horses ran alongside us. It was an amazing feeling — to be so close to nature and to what life must have been like for our own horses in their younger years. Eventually the herd lost interest and veered away, and not wanting to outstay our welcome we turned and cantered towards the mountains rather than following them. As we fell back to a walk, I felt Jackie tense beneath me, and wasn't surprised to see a bachelor stallion on the path ahead of us as we rounded the bend. As soon as he saw us, the stallion spun and crashed through the trees before jumping a creek and coming to a halt 100 metres away. He clearly didn't feel threatened, as he stayed with us, shadowing our movements, as we continued further into the mountains, although he was always careful to keep the river between us.

Circling back, we covered plenty more land but didn't try to approach any more wild horses. We'd already been awed by being in their presence and were ready to call it a day and find our way back to the trailer. After an hour of heading in the general direction, we saw it parked in the distance. Rayna and Smith, who had been left behind, were still relaxed in their stalls with plenty of hay and water left. The stock truck had only one partition, allowing us to leave the horses untied, and since it was roomy enough for the horses to turn around we hadn't been worried about leaving them in the trailer; with wild stallions around, it certainly wouldn't have been safe to have left them tied up outside.

Top
Vicki touching Rayna for the first time.

Bottom
Our first sighting of wild Mustangs in the Sulphur Mountains of Utah.

Overlooking Horseshoe
Bend in Arizona.

CHAPTER 11

Cowgirls and canyons

Riding in Bryce Canyon National Park, one of the most picturesque places we found during our time in America.

Our next trip was to Bryce Canyon — we'd heard it was a stunning ride and was one we were most excited about. We'd been told to take the horses down into the amphitheatre to ride among the hoodoos, strange pillars of rock left standing by the forces of erosion. Like so much of our road trip, though, there was little planning, and it wasn't until we got there that we found there was limited access to ride in the National Park and that bookings were both essential and limited. Pleading ignorance, we explained that we were from New Zealand and were only in the area for the day; they finally said we could ride if we returned in two hours. As a thunderstorm was looming, we first headed back into town to explore the tourist shops while the horses stayed on the trailer, sheltered from the heavy downpour.

When the rain eased we went back into the park and headed to the assigned area to unload and saddle up. Soon we were following a path along the road, before crossing over and riding past the area where the trail horses and mules stood waiting for tourists to ride them. The path eventually opened out to one of the most scenic views we'd ever encountered. The view from the top of the amphitheatre was breathtaking, and we drew our Mustangs to a stop to appreciate it — without a doubt it was one of the most picturesque locations we'd found in America. Excited about exploring it further, we urged the horses down the steep incline and into the heart of Bryce Canyon.

The path down was steep and winding; only occasionally would we find an area flat enough to trot or canter on, and each time we made sure there were no hikers in sight. The area was open to both people and horses and we were careful to respect others. When we caught up to paid clients enjoying a trail ride we slotted in behind, holding our Mustangs to a slower walk than they were accustomed to, in order not to overtake the others. We listened as the guide ahead talked about the history of the area and cracked a few jokes, and when the path was finally wide enough for us to pass, we thanked him before carrying on.

There were two major trails ahead, and apparently it was the longer ride to the Peekaboo Trail that couldn't be missed. Reaching the start of the trail, we cantered our Mustangs up the switchbacks, gaining plenty of altitude. Occasionally the path narrowed or became too steep and we'd come back to a walk, letting the horses rest for a while. The hoodoos ranged in size from just a few centimetres to 150 feet (45 metres) at their tallest, and, in places where they were impassable, tunnels had been carved into the rock. It was Bragg and Smith's first major ride on steep tracks, but both were sure-footed and reliable; they were proving to be sturdy types and we were impressed by the work the inmates had done with them.

We made it to the halfway point and were pleasantly surprised to find an area to water the horses, including rails to tie them up to. Making use of the facilities, we rested the horses before heading back down the narrow and steep tracks that weaved between the towering sandstone formations. At the bottom we debated briefly which was the correct track to take, and turned right. Soon a path flattened out and we cantered along, laughing and sharing stories, but 30 minutes later we came to a locked gate. Realising that we had gone the wrong way, we turned our Mustangs around and headed back the way we had come — a solid hour wasted. By the time we were back on the main trail the tourist group was ahead of us again, and we crawled behind them at a painfully slow walk. Ahead, we heard one of the clients asking why we were wearing helmets, and another lady replying that we must be beginners.

The next thing I knew, I was walking on the ground beside Jackie instead of riding her. She'd spooked when my jacket, which had been tied around my waist, became loose and fell to the ground. Relieved that I'd landed on my feet I hurriedly reached for her reins, but Jackie, startled by my sudden dismount, evaded me and darted away through the shrubs. Looking like the beginner the clients had mistaken us for — because who else falls off at a walk, in a straight line, and on a flat surface? — it took me five minutes to catch and re-mount Jackie. The guide told us off for disrupting the trail ride, asking us to keep careful control of our horses, and feeling thoroughly chastened I fell back into line.

We made it almost to the end without further mishap, the guide leading, with seven clients walking sedately behind, followed by the five of us on our Mustangs. But when Alexa reached up to remove her hoodie, she startled Coyote, who leapt forward, rushing up behind Jackie and Digit and causing both to leap forward, in turn startling the trail horses and mules. Beginner riders were jostled in their saddles and several nearly fell as the guide and the riders frantically fought to regain control. We were understandably unpopular with the guide! Despite the mishaps, though, Bryce Canyon scored as one of our favourite rides so far.

As we headed back to the rodeo grounds to yard the horses and check on Rayna and Parker, we tried to decide whether we'd enter the rodeo that evening. Although the mares had been ridden for just over three hours, the opportunity to enter the Barrel Race — inside an arena and in front of a crowd — was too good to miss. We agreed that they could handle working around barrels for 40 seconds; we weren't planning to go fast, so they would only need a five-minute warm-up.

We headed into town to enter at the hotel. Making a spontaneous decision, we entered not only the Barrel Race with Parker, Digit and Jackie (Coyote wasn't ready to handle the atmosphere), but also the bull-riding — all of us except Kirsty had tossed this idea around for some time as something to cross off the bucket list. After throwing together a quick meal of pasta (with a few stray pieces of hay mixed in) on the camping stove, we quickly saddled up. Although we weren't appropriately dressed for a rodeo and looked like the most English cowgirls of all time, the organisers were happy to make an exception; they were amused that we'd entered the Open Bull Ride and were trying to do the Barrel Race on wild horses with less than 25 rides behind them.

Jackie was the first to go, and since she'd warmed up beautifully I was quietly confident. Although she wouldn't be fast and I was planning to trot for the first two barrels, I was sure she'd be willing. How wrong I was. At the gate she froze, having caught sight of the grandstands filled with people and the bulls being loaded into the chutes, and it took almost a minute just to get her to the first barrel. From there we hesitantly made it to the next one, and the next, and when we finally rounded the last barrel she cantered back to the gate, eager to return to the safety of her friends. Mortified, but now aware of just how much practice the horses would need before the Extreme Mustang Makeover, I watched Vicki have her go; Parker was even worse than Jackie. By the time Digit entered the arena, our expectations were so low that we were actually impressed. Although hesitant, she trotted around the first two barrels before cantering home — the most relaxed of all our horses. Only two others competed, both locals — a 10-year-old who won it in convincing style, with Digit placing second, followed by a five-year-old who had trotted around all the barrels. Due to the lack of competition Jackie had placed fourth ahead of Parker, and I headed to the office to collect my winnings; it certainly wasn't anything to brag about.

Within seconds of the last horse leaving the arena, they announced that the Open Bull Ride was beginning, and we tied our horses and dashed to the chutes to get ready. Back-protectors and helmets were adjusted to fit, and we clustered around, listening attentively to the cowboys who were offering advice on how to hold the rope, how to position our bodies and how to mentally get the courage to hop onto the bull. Alexa was first up, and with the most mellow personality of all of us it didn't surprise me that she looked unfazed while she sat on the bull in the chute. Waiting patiently, she gripped the rope and when the gate opened she kept herself relaxed. The bull wasn't in a feral mood, more or less cantering from the chute with the occasional roller-coaster thrown in; Alexa fell off in under 8 seconds when the bull turned sharply to the right. Next up was Vicki, who had drawn a feisty red bull with a mean personality. When the gates opened it meant business — turning, spinning and bucking as it fought to dislodge its rider. Lasting for 7.3 seconds, she was the highest-scored rider of the night, and when the bull finally dislodged her she flipped through the air and landed on her feet.

I was up next, and was cautious after watching Vicki's ride. As soon as my legs were on either side of the bull, he spun his head trying to push me off his back and then tried to ram me into the sides of the chute. Panicking, I reminded myself to breathe and nodded for them to open the chute — I knew it wasn't going to go well and wanted it over as quickly as possible. Within metres of the gate the bull bucked,

Top
Jackie, Parker and Digit waiting for the Barrel Race at Bryce Canyon Rodeo.

Bottom
Vicki lasted for 7.3 seconds in the Open Bull Ride, the best time of the night.

and, prepared for the worst, I took both hands off the rope, threw them up in the air and bailed, throwing myself as far from the bull as I could — effectively surrendering. Vicki and Amanda laughed at how useless I'd been, but I was still proud — it took guts to even enter and at least I'd made it into the arena, even if I'd only lasted 2.3 seconds.

Last up was Amanda, the instigator in our decision to ride bulls, and since she'd been the highest-ranked female on the mechanical bucking bull at Fieldays she had high expectations. Unfortunately, her practice on a mechanical bull wasn't any help, and she barely made it out of the chute before the bull turned and she was thrown after 2.7 seconds. Disappointed, she vowed to try again some time in the future and we headed back to the trailer to set up camp for the evening.

Within minutes, however, the sky filled with lightning and storm clouds threatened. With the stock trailer providing insufficient shelter, we tried tying tarpaulins over the roof and down the sides to keep us dry, but if the rain was as relentless as we feared it would be, the night would be both wet and cold. Instead, we called ahead to where we'd organised to keep the horses in Mount Carmel Junction and, as they were happy for us to arrive in the dark and use their paddock a day early, we loaded in record time and headed south.

An hour down the road the storm clouds opened and the rain poured down, as sudden as it was heavy. With all of our bags and suitcases on the back of the truck, for want of room in the trailer, we pulled over, grabbed everything that needed to stay dry and clambered back into the truck with everything piled to the roof on top of us. Barely able to see over it all, we settled down and closed our eyes, sleeping the final hour away while Vicki drove. Awaking with a start, we found we'd pulled into a driveway and Vicki was parking at the entrance to the paddock. Ed, the owner, was waiting for us with a flashlight to show us where to put the horses. The rain had finally stopped but the pitch-black darkness made it impossible to see the fences. Knowing how important it was for the horses to know where the boundaries were, we walked the perimeter leading them while shining a light on the wire fence. It was the first time that the Mustangs had been contained behind wire, and with the main interstate bordering the pasture we were cautious. At the far end we found a section by the road that had fallen to the ground and we grabbed ropes to pull it upright and repair it enough to contain the horses for the night.

Satisfied, although knowing it wasn't ideal, we headed back to the trailer. Concerned, Ed asked where we were planning to spend the night, and when we said (with false bravado) that the trailer was practical and comfortable, he shook his head and offered us the use of his guest sleep-out. With more rain on the way and reluctant to spend additional money on a hotel room, we thanked him and followed him back to his house to meet his wife and settle into our rooms. By midnight, we were fast asleep.

THE NEXT MORNING WE SLEPT IN, enjoying the novelty of clean beds and showers — the first we'd had in days. It certainly beat bathing under a cold hose. By midday, we were feeling rested and in need of adventure. Since the horses were tired from their activities the day before, we gave them the day off and headed into Zion National Park for a hike. Although only a few hours from Bryce Canyon, the sandstone formations at Zion were completely different. Cream, pink and red cliffs towered thousands of feet into the sky, unlike anything we'd ever seen. Following Ed's advice, we decided to tackle The Narrows, and spent hours hiking up the river that ran along the bottom of the famed slot canyon. Drenched but happy, we made our way back to Mount Carmel Junction, fed the horses just before dark and headed to the Thunderbird Restaurant for dinner. Ed owned it and had offered us half-price meals — I think he was feeling sorry for the five straggly New Zealanders who had turned up on his doorstep in the middle of the night.

We rose before sunrise the next morning, with plans to return to Zion to attempt Angels Landing before it got too hot. On the way we stopped to feed the Mustangs, tossing them hay over the fence. Although it was still dark we could see the shadowy forms of the horses approaching — except for one that stayed in the middle of the paddock. Worried, we opened the gate and made our way over to the still horse; it was Rayna. Her injured leg was healing nicely and was still bandaged, but as we approached we realised that she'd injured her other foreleg and was holding it off the ground. While I held Rayna still, Alexa, Amanda and Kirsty brought over the vet supplies and Vicki set to work disinfecting the wound and assessing the extent of the injury. Since it was a Sunday, and we were hours from the closest town, we treated the wound as best as we could, bandaged it so that it couldn't get knocked or dirty and gave her a painkiller; we'd take her to the vet first thing the next morning. The wound needed additional treatment but it wasn't life-threatening and waiting a day wouldn't affect its healing.

With Rayna stabilised, we continued on our way. Angels Landing is reputed to be one of the most dangerous hikes in the world, and it wasn't until we got halfway up that we realised why. The first hour was exhausting, but not hazardous; slowly gaining altitude along a path following the Virgin River. From there the trail got steeper, and we continued to climb as we conquered a series of 21 switchbacks, the last hurdle before the lookout point. Hundreds of people lay haphazardly over the rocks, recovering from the rigorous climb, and it was obviously the turning-back point for most people. The brave and foolhardy, however, pushed on to the summit at the top of Angels Landing. Knowing that this was a once-in-a-lifetime experience, we continued on.

The path got narrower, and on either side it dropped over a thousand feet (300 metres) to the river below. Support chains were anchored along the route, but even with their help the path was dangerous and crowded; with so many safety issues, there is no way this hike would have been legal in New Zealand. We finally reached the top, and although exhausted stopped to appreciate the marvellous views. Returning down the mountain was just as dangerous, but once we got past the chained section, the rest was much easier and we ran along, trying to get to the bottom as quickly as possible. Tired but proud of ourselves, we ducked off the main track, slid down a bank and jumped into the river with all our clothes on, happy to float downstream rather than walk the last kilometre back to the car park.

We were back with the horses by lunch-time and relieved to find Rayna no worse. Although stiff and sore, she was happy enough and ate the feed we'd brought. We then headed inside to sleep the afternoon away. It was good to have had two days without riding and we'd enjoyed our time in Zion without the horses; a nice mental break. We took them out the next morning, saddling up early and following Ed's directions to one of Utah's most famous slot canyons. Riding the horses into the entrance, we went as far as we could before it became impassable on horseback; the canyon essentially narrowed into a cave, only accessible to climbers wanting to delve into the heart of the rock face. It was a breathtaking place and we felt lucky to have experienced it.

Not long afterwards we were on the road, en route to the vet clinic. Although there had been no appointments available, we were prepared to wait on the off-chance that the vet could administer the drugs — Vicki was happy to tidy the wound and dress it if they were too pressed for time. After grazing the horses for hours in the heat, Rayna was finally able to be seen. Once she was sedated, the vet set to work tidying up the cut; it was deep, with the bone on her foreleg exposed. Cutting off the excess skin caused it to bleed heavily and it took some time before the blood flow stemmed and Vicki was able to bandage the leg. After stocking up on vet supplies, we reloaded the horses and headed south. We were only two hours from the Grand Canyon and were hoping to find yards along the way so we could hike without the horses, then drive back and collect them to ride along the rim the following day.

After an hour of driving we started looking for a farm or yards, but with no luck. Soon we were in the Kaibab National Forest, which bordered the Grand Canyon National Park, with no chance of finding somewhere to stay. We considered driving back to the town with the vet clinic, but not only was it getting dark but also back-tracking seemed pointless. Deciding to continue on, and at least watch the sunset over the Grand Canyon, we kept driving. By now low on petrol, and unsure where the next town was, we called into a tiny petrol station in the Kaibab Forest. On hearing our accents, the lady at the counter asked where we were from and what we were doing, so I briefly shared our story. Hoping she'd know the local area, I asked her if she knew of anywhere within an hour's drive with yards; for the first time, there was a very real possibility that

Riding the horses through a
hidden slot canyon near Zion
National Park in Utah.

the horses would have to stay on the trailer overnight. Despite thinking long and hard she came up with nothing, and I thanked her, paid for the fuel and left. As I climbed into the truck she dashed out after us — I'd forgotten my card — and as she handed it back she said she'd heard of an abandoned cabin in the woods which had corrals, which might be worth a try.

Directing us back the way we'd come she told us to drive for about 10 minutes, before taking a poorly marked gravel road and following it to the cabin. Her tip proved to be a godsend, and 15 minutes later we were scouting out dilapidated yards in desperate need of repair. For the next half-hour we collected branches from the woods and tied them in place to reinforce the rotting poles. Worried about the Mustangs escaping — into over a million acres of National Park — we strung a roll of plastic sheeting that we had found in the cabin around the perimeter of the yards to make the fences higher and more visible. Confident that they would now hold the horses, we unloaded and settled them before driving to the rim of the Grand Canyon, 20 minutes down the road, to watch the sunset; a truly spectacular sight. As there was no water at the cabin we stopped by a pond on our way back, filled buckets of water and drove the last 5 kilometres slowly so as not to spill any of the muddy water. It would have to tide the horses over for the night.

It was a lovely evening so we set up camp in the grass, spreading our mattresses and blankets over a tarpaulin on the ground; much better than sleeping on the dirty floor of the trailer. Not totally convinced about the comfort or the temperature of sleeping under the stars, however, I opted to use the back seat of the truck again, even though it was too narrow for me to lie flat and I had to sleep with my legs tucked up.

THE NEXT MORNING, WE WERE BACK ON the road. We'd accidentally come to the North Rim of the Grand Canyon, instead of the more scenic South Rim, and there wasn't much to do here. Not being able to justify a four-hour drive around to the other side, we planned to head north, weaving our way up through Arizona and Colorado before returning to Wyoming; this was the most southern part of what would become a 5000-kilometre road trip. Before we loaded up, though, we decided to make the most of the Kaibab Forest by going for a ride through the trees. There were plenty of felled trees that made great jumps and we cantered along the tracks, jumping logs as we went. Some were as high as 3 feet (90 centimetres) — a pretty good effort on such inexperienced horses, especially for Kirsty and I, who rode bareback. Although it was only the mares' third time jumping, and the prison geldings' first time, they were all naturally talented and again we were impressed by their sensible natures and athletic ability.

Not far from the Kaibab Forest, Vicki stopped for fuel, and when we were ready to go she tossed me the keys and told me to drive. Thinking — or hoping — she was joking, I threw them back, but she let them fall to the ground and hopped in the back seat. Worried, I slid into the driver's seat and asked a few fundamental questions about how to tow a trailer; but rather than offer words of wisdom, Vicki shrugged her shoulders said I was a big girl and would figure it out, and closed her eyes to sleep. Hoping for the best, and trusting the advice from Alexa in the passenger seat — who'd had even less driving experience than me — I started the truck and eased onto the road, careful to stay on the right side. Two minutes later, at the first intersection, I didn't pull out wide enough to allow for the eight-horse stock trailer and we had a near-miss with an oncoming vehicle. Stressed out, I drove slowly; it was annoying for everyone behind me, but since my first time driving was on a steep, winding road, I was more concerned with our own welfare than about keeping other drivers happy. Keeping well below the speed limit, we slowly made our way west through Arizona. Unused to driving, I asked Vicki to have a turn so I could rest, but she said that she'd managed to drive thousands of kilometres so far, and it was ridiculous that I couldn't even manage a few hours.

To stop myself falling asleep at the wheel, I pulled over at some rock huts to stretch my legs. Alexa and the others went off to explore the primal dwellings while I rested in the shade. Returning to the truck I asked Alexa for the keys, and she looked at me and said that she'd locked it internally, assuming I'd taken the keys with me. We quickly realised

Amanda teaching Bragg to jump, just nine days after we bought him, over a felled log near the abandoned cabin we found in the Kaibab Forest.

none of us had the keys; I glanced in the window to find them hanging in the ignition. Vicki took great delight in pointing out that we'd made it more than halfway through our time in America with her driving and no mishaps, and already in just a couple of hours I'd almost shredded tyres on the kerb and locked us out of the truck.

Fortunately, we had cell-phone reception, but the closest locksmith's was hours away and it was going to cost hundreds of dollars for them to come out and break us into the truck. After a little brainstorming we came to the conclusion that it would be cheaper to break a window than pay for a locksmith, and we sat on the back of the truck deliberating which window would be the cheapest to replace. We'd finally settled on the small window at the back and were discussing the best way to break it when we heard Vicki yelling something about the police. Looking up, we saw her pointing at an approaching car, and we sprinted to the road to flag it down.

The police officer felt sorry for us, and although he didn't have the tools needed to open the door, he called the closest park ranger for help. Half an hour later, and after promising that we wouldn't hold him liable if our car door was damaged, he had the door open in minutes. Thanking them both — they had saved us time as well as money — we got under way again. A few hours later we arrived in Page, a large city near Lake Powell and Horseshoe Bend. Sadly, horses weren't allowed in the lake, so we settled them at the rodeo grounds and worked them in the arena that afternoon, getting them used to walking and trotting on the lead while we stayed beside their shoulder, one of the required elements of the Handling and Conditioning class, and then getting them to walk under and over tarpaulins and a sheet of orange plastic we'd acquired on our travels.

By early evening it had started raining and we used the tarps to cover the sides of the trailer, cutting up feed sacks to patch any spots that were still leaking. We'd paid over US$100 to keep our seven horses at the rodeo grounds overnight, and again couldn't justify the added expense of a hotel room. We made our beds and fell asleep, and were relieved to wake up the next morning only slightly damp — the rain had lasted for only a couple of hours. Ready to explore, we returned to the lake to swim without the horses, first on one of the sandy beaches, then jumping off the rocks near the head of the dam, before showering in the public bathrooms.

From there we headed to McDonald's for some much-needed internet and power, and spent the next couple of hours charging laptops and phones, while answering emails and checking how the second episode of *Keeping Up With the Kaimanawas* had gone. For the second week it was the highest-rated evening show across every network — one in every eight New Zealanders had watched the first two episodes — and we were so relieved that we were out of the country. We were just small-town and country girls, and when we'd agreed to do the series I don't think we'd really considered that we might become well-known or that the show would reach such a large audience.

The next morning we woke late, had lunch in town, and then drove the horses down to the Horseshoe Bend trail for a ride, hoping to continue on to Monument Valley afterwards. Unloading the horses in a crowded car park, we jumped on bareback and weaved our way through the cars, bypassing the main track where hundreds of people were hiking, and trotting up the hill along an old 4WD track before going cross-country. It didn't take long to reach Horseshoe Bend, and we rode our horses right to the edge of the rocky cliffs, in awe of the view. It was remarkable that the Colorado River had gouged out such a deep and spectacular twist in the river, and even more amazing to know that further downstream it was responsible for creating the Grand Canyon.

After taking photos we turned back towards the trailer, cantering back the way we'd come. The Mustangs were all quite reliable now, and it didn't take long before they were loaded and we were back on the road, although by now it was late evening and it was unlikely that we would get to Monument Valley before dark. Again I was driving because Vicki refused to; at times I questioned whether I was being punished for something, since she knew how much I hated to drive, but I couldn't figure out what I could have done to be subjected to these endless hours behind the wheel. Finally, she confessed that it was because her leg was seizing up following the fall she'd had off Red weeks earlier; she'd not told us before because she didn't want us to worry.

Once again, with no forward planning, we decided to stop anywhere along the way where we found suitable yards. We were planning to ride the horses at sunrise through the vast sandstone buttes that towered 1000 feet (300 metres) above the valley floor. Five years earlier I had watched the sunrise over Monument Valley and it had been one of highlights of that trip, so I was keen to do it again.

By 10.30 p.m. it was pitch-black and we were getting worried — there was no cell-phone reception and we were in the middle of nowhere, not even a farmhouse in sight. However, suddenly we passed an arena with high fencing; as this was probably our best hope we pulled over, did a U-turn and headed back. The house was up a long, rough driveway, and when we finally bumped to a stop over the unforgiving terrain we were greeted by vicious-looking dogs that were barking aggressively. Amanda and Alexa slowly got out, careful not to rile the dogs up further — the fact that they were even willing to risk it showed how desperate we were.

They were met at the door by an older Native American; when they asked whether we could put the horses in his arena overnight, he broke into a grin, said we would be more than welcome and jumped in his truck to show us the way. We put the lights of both trucks on full beam to light up the arena, and quickly fed and watered the horses. The man's wife joined us and couldn't have been more hospitable, offering to let us put our mattresses on their garage floor for shelter overnight. But with only a few hours until we had to continue driving to Monument Valley, we decided that the trailer would be more efficient.

With only three hours of sleep ahead of us, Kirsty jumped in the front seat to save setting up a bed in the trailer, and we stayed up talking for a bit. Bright lights lit up the sky, snaking their way in an unfamiliar pattern across the horizon. Although we joked that it was either the strangest lightning storm we'd ever seen or the Northern Lights, we were equally convinced that there were more plausible explanations. It wasn't until weeks later that someone asked if we'd seen the rare viewing of the Aurora Borealis dancing across the sky, and we realised that we had indeed seen the Northern Lights. They hadn't appeared that far south in more than a decade; normally they are only viewable in countries near the Arctic Circle.

Riding the Mustangs at sunrise
at Monument Valley in Arizona.

CHAPTER 12

Mustangs in town — and country

Ordering breakfast at the drive-through.

We woke in the dark, first catching Parker, Coyote, Bragg and Digit, before attempting Jackie, Smith and Rayna, who were a little more difficult in a large group, especially at night. Driving the 40 minutes towards Monument Valley, we stopped well before the Navajo Tribal Park so that we could film and photograph the horses silhouetted against the sandstone formations. We were hoping to get photos for this book's cover, as well as footage for a trailer. Although Kirsty and Alexa had proven quite talented behind the cameras when needed, getting the light right in the sunrise shoot would be quite challenging, so we got them to ride Jackie and Bragg as body doubles. Not only were they part of our adventure, but with the backlighting it would also be impossible to tell who was riding the horses anyway. It wasn't long before the sun broke above the buttes and sunlight lit up the valley floor as the horses cantered towards us. The lighting was perfect; with our shots captured, we loaded the horses with their saddles still on and headed for the Navajo Tribal Park, hoping to ride through. Unfortunately we weren't able to get permission to ride on Navajo land, and turned back the way we had come. Keeping a good eye out for possible places to ride we passed many buttes, but none rivalled the beauty of those we'd already seen. Soon they were long behind us and we had reached the town of Kayenta.

The golden arches of McDonald's could be seen from miles away, and as we were hungry we decided to ride the horses through the small town. It would be great exposure for them, with moving vehicles and the busy-ness of town life. We parked around the corner from McDonald's in a vacant car park; Smith and Rayna were left on the trailer with food and water, and we rode along the footpaths, crossed over a ditch and made our way to the drive-through line, hoping they would serve us breakfast on horseback. We'd done this successfully in New Zealand years earlier, and were interested to see whether we'd get lucky again. The horses stood patiently in line between two trucks while around us some locals approached to photograph Mustangs in the drive-through.

Our order got taken, and Alexa rode to the next window to collect our food, passing it over to each of us. Amused we rode off, holding the reins in one hand and McMuffins in the other while balancing Parfaits on the front of the saddles. Not ready to stop yet, we passed the trailer and headed for the far side of town — the local high school had a huge banner saying 'Home of the Mustangs' which we wanted to take a photo in front of. Once our food was gone we picked up the pace, cantering along the grass verge; the horses were curious and unfazed by everything they were seeing. We spotted a children's playground with no one in it, and since it was still not yet 7 a.m. we crossed the road to ride the horses through, going under slides, in between swings and under a rock-climbing arch. It was a great test for the horses, who would have to work through a trail course as part of the Extreme Mustang Makeover. Adjoining the playground was a skate park, and since that was also empty we rode the horses onto the jumps, getting them to stand with all four hooves on the raised platforms; some walked straight on and others took some time, unsure about the clang of their shoes against the metal structures.

After over an hour spent playing with random obstacles, we headed for the trailer, forgoing the ride to the high school since it was nearing school hours. Cantering along the sandy track beside the footpath, I was bringing up the rear, lagging well behind the others. Behind me I heard dogs barking furiously and turned to see three pit bulls tearing up the track behind us. Jackie tensed and I urged her forward, galloping to catch up to the others in the hope that the dogs would be deterred by a larger group of horses. Realising something was wrong, the others slowed to a walk and turned their horses as I drew to halt beside them. Faced with a wall of horses, the dogs slunk off with their tails between their legs.

Since we'd parked beside a car wash, we put coins into one of the bays, led the horses in and water-blasted the sweat from their coats. We got a few strange looks from the people washing their vehicles, but kept at it until all five horses were clean. Before we had a chance to load, the threatening storm clouds burst and we got drenched.

The rain didn't last for long, though, and an hour later we pulled into the Four Corners, where Arizona, Utah, Colorado and New Mexico meet — the only place in America where four states join. It was a touristy

Top
Bragg in the playground.

Bottom
Jackie and Coyote on the skateboard ramps.

place, with lots of handmade Navajo jewellery and souvenirs to buy, and it was interesting to get an insight into the people who lived on the reservation. So many people saw them as both victims and a curiosity, and were taking photos of the Navajo people selling their wares; it wasn't until a beautiful lady selling jewellery asked someone not to take her photo, and explained why, that we realised just how misrepresented these proud people are in popular culture.

From the Four Corners we crossed the state line into Colorado; our next stop was the Mesa Verde National Park to explore the ancient cliff dwellings. Once in Cortez, the closest town, the search for a place to keep the horses began. Our first stop was the rodeo grounds, but they were hosting a Pro Rodeo over the next two days and there were no yards available. They pointed us towards the Livestock Auctions and we headed there to see if they would let us stay. Alexa and I went inside to enquire about using the yards, and were greeted by a lovely, but rather absent-minded, gentleman who was enthusiastic about meeting foreigners riding wild Mustangs around America. He agreed to give us the use of the yards for as long as we needed them.

Just as we were about to head outside to unload the horses, a guy walked in to collect a cheque for a bull he had sold at auction. We were quickly introduced by the livestock manager, who rattled on about what we were up to. Half-joking, the guy, who introduced himself as Ricky, said he'd take us to round up cattle if we wanted a true Wild West experience; we said we were interested, but he obviously didn't take us seriously. As he was about to drive off in his truck, we realised that we had no contact details and sprinted after him, telling him that we were keen and asking him when and where he needed us. Surprised that we really were interested — and perhaps a little worried about how rideable our wild horses were — he said he'd meet us here early the next morning, and that we needed to have our horses loaded on the trailer and ready to go at 8 a.m. We then asked him if he knew where the best place was to buy hay; laughing, he told us he was a hay contractor and he'd bring us 20 bales the following morning as a thank-you for helping him search for his cattle.

THE NEXT DAY THE WEATHER FORECAST DIDN'T look promising, but always game for an adventure we got ready and hoped for the best. Five minutes down the road, our truck overheated and I eased it to the side of the road. Luckily Ricky, who was ahead of us, noticed that we'd stopped and pulled over to wait for us. After realising we had a problem, he came back to help and it quickly became apparent that the engine needed some coolant. While Ricky headed to the local garage to buy some, we unloaded our Mustangs and reloaded them into Ricky's trailer; our engine would need to cool before we could drive it again. Leaving our truck on the side of the road, we all continued on to the forest. As we drove, Ricky filled us in on the cattle we would be mustering; there were about 44 pairs (around 80 cows and calves) lost in a 10,000-acre forest from when they'd been droving them from winter to summer pasture the week before.

Amazed and a little curious about how he'd lost cattle, we kept asking questions and soon the entire story unfolded. Ricky's good friend, renowned horseman Pat Parelli, had come down with a few friends to help muster the cattle, but they hadn't known that another rancher was also droving his cattle the same day. The two herds had collided in the forest, mixing up almost 3000 cattle. Pat and Joseph, his right-hand man, were able to sort most of the cattle, cutting the two herds into separate groups. The process took a couple of hours, and with limited men to hold the remaining cattle they'd lost about 250 pairs into the surrounding trees. Although they'd returned to the forest to search for the lost cattle, they'd only found just over 200 pairs.

A week had passed, and there was a lot of dense forest to search. Splitting into two groups we canvassed the forest floor, trying to cover as much ground as possible. Unfortunately, the cattle hadn't stuck together, and every half-hour we'd find a few more. As our motley collection grew in numbers they became easier to control; when there'd been just one or two it had required a lot of effort to keep them moving in the same direction, but once we had five, then 10, pairs they became easier to manage.

Kirsty had ridden bareback to avoid damaging one of our good jumping saddles if it started raining, and sure enough it soon did. Drenched to the bone, we continued on, slowly adding to our growing numbers. Occasionally we would leave the group to check a gully for cattle; once Vicki was gone for half an hour, returning with another 10 pairs. Smith was proving to be a remarkable stock horse — he was confident out on the trials and adept at working the cattle. Another gully lay to the right of us, and Ricky, Kirsty and I headed down it. About 10 minutes later we saw a calf, and circled wide to get behind it and push it back to the others. Rather than holding its ground the calf turned and fled, and hoping to cut it off Ricky galloped his horse to the left. When he finally stopped his headlong flight, with the calf now moving in the right direction, he turned in surprise to find us flanking him. His gallop through trees, down hills, over ditches and through thick scrub had been so frantic that he was startled to find us on his tail — especially Kirsty who was riding bareback. Impressed both with our riding and with how responsive our Mustangs were after only 58 days of handling, he said that we were some of the best horsemen he had ever seen; high praise indeed from someone who rides and trains with one of the world's most respected horsemen.

Four hours after we started, we finally got the cattle through the gates onto the new grazing; we'd found 41 of the 44 pairs, which was a remarkable effort considering how widely they had been scattered through the forest. Back at our truck, the coolant worked a treat and we drove it back to the stockyards, unloaded the horses from Ricky's trailer and settled them before going off to find a hotel for the night. We were far too wet and tired to have another uncomfortable night in the trailer, and were in desperate need of both a shower and a washing machine.

Over the next couple of days we drove the truck a few times with no issues, including into Mesa Verde National Park and to watch the Pro Rodeo, and were hopeful that it was okay. Assuming that it had only overheated because it had run out of water, we now loaded the horses to head north through Colorado. Less than five minutes into our drive, however, warning lights came on, and when we pulled to a stop the engine was steaming; it seemed as if the heavy load of the horses was causing something to fail. Calling Ricky, we explained our problem and he offered us the use of his paddock for a few days while we got it sorted; it was great having someone local to turn to for help. Since Cortez was a small town with few mechanics, Ricky was unsure how long the truck would take to fix and offered us an intriguing option. Rather than staying at his property, which had no facilities for training horses — now crucial with the competition only a month away — he asked us whether we would like to visit the Parelli Ranch, which was set up with arena, jumps, obstacles, trails and cross-country courses.

It sounded like a phenomenal opportunity — Pat Parelli is renowned for training horses using natural horsemanship, and we were definitely interested to meet him. A quick phone-call was all it took, and the next morning we piled into Ricky's truck, which was towing our horses and trailer, while Vicki followed in our truck (which again didn't overheat since it wasn't towing). Almost two hours later we arrived in Pagosa Springs at the Parelli Ranch, and couldn't contain our smiles as we looked around — we were excited to watch and learn as much as we could during our visit. Ricky had explained that Pat didn't suffer fools gladly and we had one chance to impress him; if we did, we could stay at the property until the truck was ready, rather than returning to Ricky's that afternoon.

Pat, his wife, Linda, and their team met us, and after being invited to ride with them we saddled our Mustangs and joined them to bring in cattle from pasture. Ricky had a cutting horse training with Pat, and we were bringing the cattle into a huge round arena so that Ricky could practise. While Ricky, Pat and Joseph took turns working the cattle, the rest of us lined the round pen to keep them off the edges. Every time one of the cattle approached, we'd block them by reining back or doing a roll-back (a turn on the haunches to change direction, improving the horse's lateral work). It was a good test of patience for the horses, one that Bragg failed — standing and waiting were not his favourite pastimes and he grew agitated. Pat was quick to notice and suggested that Amanda allow the bored horse to wander, while the rest of us moved over to fill the gap she'd left behind. Each of us had turns with the cattle, not cutting, but rather getting the horses familiar with riding into a herd and seeing whether they would latch on and follow one. Some, like Parker and Coyote, were naturally engaged and followed the cattle instinctively, but the others didn't understand the purpose of the exercise.

The arena was set up in a paddock scattered with cross-country fences and obstacles, and once we were finished with the cattle we headed out to play. After our practice on the playground in Arizona, the Mustangs were brave and willing to tackle the bridges, tyres and obstacles — walking under, on and through things as well as half-passing over logs and jumping into a log-box before doing a turn on the haunches and jumping out again. We then progressed to jumping bigger fences; initially trotting, then cantering, over logs and combinations, working our way up to 3-foot (90-centimetre) fences.

Pleased with the horses, we headed back to the trailer to unsaddle, stoked to hear that we were invited to stay until the truck was fixed. Pat and Linda asked us where we were sleeping, and when we pointed to the trailer and said it was set up, they looked at us askance and offered us the use of a rustic cabin and the choice between pasture or yards for the horses. Choosing the pasture, we headed down to release the horses, optimistically hoping that they would let us catch them again — it was the largest paddock they had been let loose in, and the grass was so high we couldn't see their legs. Once they were settled we headed to the cabin, realising that it would be the first time we'd each had a normal bed since we'd left Wyoming six weeks earlier.

We were going out to dinner with Ricky and Joseph, and on the way dropped the truck off at the mechanic's. Soon we were eating Mexican food for the first time, and chatting like old friends, even though we'd only known Ricky for a few days and Joseph a couple of hours. From there Joseph dropped us off at the cabin, and Ricky headed back to Cortez. We were truckless until it was fixed, but were incredibly lucky to have landed ourselves in a place where we had everything we could possibly need to train our horses, and like-minded people to spend our time with.

TOP
Vicki and Parker
working with cattle at
the Parelli Ranch.

MIDDLE
Vicki and Rayna on
the Parelli Ranch
obstacle course.

BOTTOM
Jackie and I jumping
over a log on the cross-
country course.

WITH A FEW HOURS OF DAYLIGHT LEFT, we headed down to the horses; Rayna needed her bandages changing, and Vicki was going to ride Smith. Although she'd had the least handling, Rayna was the first to be caught, but it quickly became apparent that Smith wasn't going to be easy. Hoping to simplify things, we grabbed all of the halters, planning to catch the easiest ones so they wouldn't get in the way. Kirsty soon had Digit, but the others galloped around the pasture, intent on retaining their freedom. They paused in one corner, and Amanda approached quietly to catch Bragg, who was normally the friendliest. Instead of standing, however, he spun and jumped the fence — and a rail that had rotted after the winter snowfall broke, leaving a gap in the fence. The other four turned to follow, each clearing the lower rails easily. We watched in disbelief as our Mustangs galloped up the driveway and down the races that led past the Parelli horses.

Sprinting after them, Alexa, Amanda and I ran to block their flight, and Kirsty cantered alongside on Digit; even from hundreds of metres away it was obvious that the gate leading into the million-acre National Forest was open and we frantically hoped that the horses would stop well before they realised this. In the distance, we saw our horses turn at the end of the race, then gallop through the open gate and into the dense forest. Winded, we stopped to catch our breath; we desperately needed to regroup and make a plan. Vicki had managed to keep hold of Rayna and, in the distance, we could see her safely contained in high yards. With darkness approaching and a storm threatening, we knew we had to find our Mustangs before nightfall if we had any hope of getting them back without the aid of a search party and hours of canvassing the forest floor to track their hoof-prints.

By the time we reached the gate, the heavens had opened and the unrelenting rain soon soaked us to the skin. It was already late evening, and under the towering trees there was barely enough light to see. Splitting up, we stumbled through the thick underbrush, following the skid marks of our fleeing horses, which were long out of sight. Overhead, thunder and lighting lit up the sky, and soon it was too dark to see hoof-prints; we had no idea which way the horses had gone, and knew there was a real risk that we would get lost ourselves. If we didn't find our Mustangs soon, we'd have to quit and come back at day-break. A few minutes later we heard thundering hooves, and soon the shadowy form of a horse took shape; Parker galloped towards us, circling around Digit. Although it took a while to calm the panicked animal, we soon had him caught. Not wanting to risk losing him again, Amanda led him back to the ranch while the rest of us kept searching; it was unusual for horses to split up, and we hoped that Jackie, Coyote, Smith and Bragg weren't far ahead. Heading up a steep incline, I pushed my way through thick branches, sliding on the muddy track, freezing cold and worried sick.

With relief I reached the top of the incline to see Kirsty and Digit; exhausted, I barely processed the fact that the other horses were all within sight. Standing well back in the shadow of the trees, so I wouldn't send them into flight mode again, I watched as Kirsty rode her Mustang alongside the other horses; once she was among them, she dismounted to halter Bragg. As soon as her feet touched the ground, however, the horses startled and retreated from her; not wanting to lose them again, she vaulted back on Digit and sat quietly watching them. These once-wild horses had just had their biggest taste of freedom for years, and being caught was the last thing they wanted. I watched to see what Kirsty's next move would be, and was impressed to see her ride up alongside Bragg again, this time reaching out to touch him while she remained mounted. Once he was calm, she threaded a rope around his neck, drew him alongside her and reached out to awkwardly halter him off Digit's back. Calling out quietly I told Kirsty to bring him to me, and carefully stepped out of the trees to take his lead. The other three were already more relaxed, and one by one Kirsty repeated the process until I held three horses. Approaching Smith, the last of them, she caught him, too. It was over. The past hour in the forest had been incredibly stressful with no guaranteed outcome, and it was with huge relief that we now stood holding the last four runaways.

Passing one of my horses to Kirsty, we moved back in the general direction we had come, hoping to find our way back to the ranch gate easily. We had a general sense of the direction and knew that we had to head downhill. The rain was still torrential; overhead, thunder rumbled and lightning intermittently lit up the sky, lighting our path. We made it down the first hill and heard Amanda and Alexa calling frantically in the distance; continuing on, we used their voices to guide us. Soon we were on top of them, and as leading two horses was a challenge on the narrow and slippery tracks we passed them a Mustang each, relieved that the end was almost in sight. Ten minutes later we were at the gate; once through it, we shut it to prevent another escape and then headed slowly back to the yards; the horses certainly weren't going back in the pasture again and would have six-foot-high fences to keep them contained overnight — at least we would know they were safe and would be able to rest easy.

We woke at day-break to blue skies and horses still safely tucked into their yards, nickering when they saw us approaching. It was as if the catastrophe of the night before had never happened. When Pat and his team arrived and heard of our misadventure they laughed, but Pat said that we were very lucky — he'd once lost horses in the forest for a week and they'd had to use helicopters to find them. Our first task now was to repair the broken rail in the pasture, and we asked where we would find a spare rail, nails and a hammer. After being pointed in the right direction we checked the rest of the fence, leaning our weight on each rail to test whether they were rotten. After counting at least 20 that needed replacing, we loaded a farm truck with rails and set to work, drilling holes and nailing them into place. We were soon exhausted in the hot morning sun — even walking up the hill to the cabin was hard work, and we arrived at the top breathless. Unsure why we were struggling, after we'd hiked Angels Landing with no issues, we joked about it with Joseph and the team, and they told us it was the altitude; apparently, working this high up in the Colorado Mountains took a while to get acclimatised to.

After working our horses through the obstacles and over the logs again, we kept ourselves busy helping around the ranch; we were interested in watching the team train their horses to cut stock, first working with a flag and then progressing to cattle. The stables and big-top arena, where our

Jackie on the tyre.

horses were based, was a Western-dominated area known as Pat's World; Linda, who rode English-style like ourselves, had her horses based at another stable block and arena, called Linda Land, beside their house. Parelli Ranch was an excellent combination of both disciplines, offering us unparalleled facilities with which to further our Mustangs' education — we were very grateful to Ricky for the introduction.

Setting up barrels and poles, we constructed jumps in the track around the arena, training the horses over showjumps for the first time since Reno; for the prison horses, it was their very first time over proper jumps. They were all wobbly and green for the first couple of attempts, but with steady legs, a reassuring voice and soft hands we were able to instil confidence in Coyote, Smith and Jackie, and they confidently tackled the jumps. By the end of the session all three had progressed from a cross to a solid line of upright barrels with a pole on top. The jump now stood at 3 foot 6 inches (1.05 metres), and one by one we cantered the horses around and jumped it. Each of them cleared it with plenty of air, again impressing us with their natural talent for jumping. While we washed the horses off, Kirsty and Vicki saddled up Digit and Parker, and they, too, showed huge scope and talent — these Mustangs, born and bred in the Wild West, certainly had their uses in the English world, and we were confident that the majority of the horses we were training were capable of top-level jumping.

Later that afternoon, Pat introduced us to his business partner, Mark, and we started talking about why we were in America, our dreams and inspirations, and our aim to improve horse welfare on a global scale. Our passion obviously shone through, and when Mark heard that we'd been travelling and living in our trailer, he knew we were both committed and willing to rough it to make our dreams a reality. He asked us to meet him at the Parelli head office the following day to show us anything and everything he could about how they'd gone from nearing bankruptcy to being a multi-million-dollar company.

There was so much to absorb that we ended up having two sessions with Mark, who was incredibly open about everything — no question was off-limits. Despite starting out with few qualifications, Mark's vision and tenacity made him a success by the age of 23; unfortunately, he became a workaholic and both his principles and his family life suffered. Then he met a young Pat Parelli, and realised that here was someone who lived by the cowboy code — if you say something you mean it, and you will do everything possible to keep your word. Mark was inspired to help Pat and Linda achieve their dream, and now he was incredibly generous in sharing his wisdom with us.

The following day, we got a call to say that the problem with our truck was only a sensor and they would have it fixed in a couple of days. The timing was perfect, and it would cost only a couple of hundred dollars to fix, which was a huge relief. Since our time at the Parelli Ranch was now coming to an end, we spent the next two days playing with the horses, teaching them to load on foreign trailers, trail-riding bareback through the forest and developing Western lateral movements which are a bit different to our normal English ones. The improvement we were seeing in our horses was huge, and in our spare time we watched the other trainers working.

On our last evening, the Parelli Ranch hosted a 'Savvy Evening', where locals could visit the ranch and watch the Parelli students working with horses. Pat invited us to do a demonstration with the Mustangs and we agreed — although it would be nerve-wracking to ride in front of others, it would be invaluable for our horses to work in a crowd atmosphere. With only a couple hours' notice we came up with a quick plan, keeping our demonstration as simple as possible — the horses had already been worked for the day, and we didn't want to do anything too tiring. Jackie, Coyote and Digit jumped and did some basic lateral work before we began working with a ball — Kirsty standing on Digit's back while we tossed it back and forth to each other.

Early on the last morning we worked the horses one last time, making the most of the facilities — the next week was going to be spent riding through National Parks, so the horses would get very little schooling. Since it was only four weeks until the EMM, it was important to make the most of the arena while we had it.

By midday we had collected the truck and driven back to the Parelli

Ranch to hook up the trailer and load the horses. Waving farewell to our generous hosts, we headed north — but after five minutes, to our despair, the truck overheated again, even worse than the first two times. Worried about driving further, we called Joseph and asked if he would be able to collect us. It seemed that the local mechanic had fixed the wrong thing and we dropped the truck back off for them to look at again. For now, our stay in Pagosa Springs was extended.

Rayna refusing to go near
the water's edge, at a lake
we stopped at on our drive
north through Colorado.

CHAPTER 13

Troublesome times

The Parelli Ranch wasn't a bad place to be stuck, and secretly we were quite pleased — we'd made great friends with Joseph, his fiancée Rachel, and Ellie, Ryan and Whitney, who worked with the horses. To fill in time and as a thank-you for having us longer than they'd planned, we spent our spare time repairing fences, replacing over a hundred rails. Our evenings were spent at karaoke, lazing in the local hot springs, or eating out with our new friends. Caton, Pat's son, got to know us well and often joked that he'd marry one of us, but that there was no way he'd ever let our kids wear 'those sissy pants or a helmet' — they'd be real cowboys with wrangler jeans and a Western hat. He was good value, and could always make us laugh.

Another two days later we got a call to say that the truck was fixed and ready to collect; they'd found an issue with the fan and had got it replaced. Time was running out before we had to be back in Wyoming for a Showtym USA Retreat we had planned, so we headed to the mechanic's that afternoon, returned to load the horses and set off again. We had over 1000 kilometres to drive and only a few days to do it in. Forty minutes down the road we came to a big mountain pass; our truck was pulling well, but halfway up it overheated again, and we were stranded. Not wanting to hassle Joseph again, even though he'd told us to call if we had issues, we flagged down a stranger and got them to look under the hood. After being told we couldn't continue to drive it, and with a 40-minute drive back to the closest town, we slowly dialled Joseph's number. Although hesitant to ask him to rescue us again, we knew he would: he is one of those rare guys who lives by the cowboy code — completely selfless and always willing to help.

An hour later we swapped the trailer onto the ranch truck, and Alexa and I piled in to keep Joseph company while the others followed behind — again the truck was fine to drive without the trailer to pull. We had lost all confidence in the mechanic's ability to fix the issue, so after settling the horses at the Parelli Ranch again, Alexa and I drove an hour south to Durango where there was a specialist Ford workshop. It was crucial that we get it fixed within two days, because we still had a full day's drive ahead of us to collect the riders who were flying in from the

East Coast and New Zealand to attend the retreat. If the truck wasn't fixed by then, we had no idea when or how we would get back in time to host them.

By mid-afternoon the Ford mechanic had a diagnosis for us, and our spirits sank even further — the water pump and front case housing needed replacing, which would cost almost US$5000. The only positive was that they had the parts and could get it fixed within our time limit. Overwhelmed, we sat down and considered our options; but realistically, we were in a terrible position. We couldn't afford a new truck and, although we hadn't budgeted for it, we had to go ahead with the repairs. Dejected, we waited for Pat to collect us from the mechanic; he'd just flown in after teaching a clinic, so the timing worked well, and we put our woes aside as we chatted with him on the drive back to the ranch.

On Monday morning, two days later, we called to ask what time our truck would be ready to collect and were met with an awkward silence; they hadn't started work on it. In fact, they'd fired the mechanic who had looked at our truck, due to incompetency, and were so short-staffed that they were well behind on work. After explaining our urgency, they promised to look at the truck and call us back within the hour. Stressed by both the financial burden and the time pressure, I was in tears: there was a very real possibility we would have to leave the Mustangs at Parelli Ranch and fly into Wyoming to host the retreat — a waste of even more money.

The phone finally rang, and with trembling fingers I picked it up and answered. Expecting the worst, I listened in shock as the mechanic updated me. After a thorough check they had found nothing wrong with the truck and had no idea how the other mechanic had got it so wrong. Most likely the original problem had been the fan, which had been fixed by the mechanic in Pagosa Springs, and the last time the truck had overheated was simply because it was such a steep mountain pass, with a heavy load, on a hot summer's day. He advised us to drive along mountain roads in the early hours of the morning while it was still cool, and said that the truck was ready to collect whenever we were ready. Confused but elated, I filled everyone in on the good news, and went to find Joseph to see if he could drive us in to collect the truck the following morning.

A film crew was arriving on the Parelli Ranch that day, however, and Joseph needed to be at work from 7 a.m. onwards. Disheartened but totally understanding, we asked around some of the other hands; but before any of them could commit, Joseph offered to drive us in at 4 a.m., with our trailer-load of horses hitched to his truck so that we wouldn't have to waste time back-tracking to the ranch; this would also allow us to get through the mountains well before the heat of the day. Feeling terrible for turning a long day into an even longer day for him, we thanked Joseph profusely — he had gone from stranger, to friend, to hero in the 10 days we'd been at the Parelli Ranch, and we knew we had a friend for life.

By 6 a.m., we had the trailer hitched up to our own truck, and after thanking Joseph again we headed north. We were taking a different route to avoid Wolf Pass; although the drive was longer, the mountains weren't as steep. The detour would take us briefly through Utah, before heading up through Colorado and into Wyoming; we had 12 hours of driving to do and less than two days to get there.

Every half-hour we stopped to let the truck cool, aware of the risk of driving it over the steep terrain. Although Ford had cleared it, there was still a possibility they'd missed something — overheating often can't be diagnosed properly without pulling apart the engine, which we'd opted not to do. We were taking a punt and could only hope that it was the right call. Four hours into our stop-and-start trip, in scorching temperatures, we decided to stop and rest the engine again — it was so hot that the air-conditioning made no difference, and was even worse with the windows down. It was the hottest day we'd encountered in America; even with bags of ice on our laps to keep us cool, we were sweating from the heat. We called into a stable complex and put the horses in stalls to rest and have something to eat and drink.

By late morning we loaded up; we were less than an hour from Arches National Park and wanted to ride the horses near there to stretch their legs. Pulling down a side road, we headed towards the red sandstone formations in the distance, parked the trailer and jumped on bareback; Rayna and Parker stayed in the trailer. The sign at the entrance outlined tracks with dinosaur fossils, and we headed down the sandy river bed in search of ancient signs of life. Our plans for a quick ride were short-lived; instead of heading back after 20 minutes, Vicki managed to convince us that we were riding on a loop and it would be much faster to keep going. What should have been a 40-minute ride was drawn out for hours after we got lost multiple times and rode over rocky outcrops for miles.

Rarely was the surface flat, and deep, impassable crevices meant that often we would have to back-track. After we'd scaled a particularly rocky cliff it was impossible to return the way we'd come, as the rocks were too slippery for us to safely retrace our steps. Instead we were faced with having to cross a hazardous man-made 'bridge' over a slot canyon: boulders had been tossed into the deep crevice and dust had been thrown into the gaps to make it possible for people to cross. The path was narrow, less than a metre wide and certainly not designed for horses; if we fell it was certain death, as the ground was 6 metres down and littered with jagged rocks. Exhausted, burnt and dehydrated from hours riding in the relentless sun, but with no option, Vicki volunteered to cross first. Urging her horse forward, she edged onto the bridge. Halfway over Smith's legs started sinking into the unstable dust — with the path being too narrow to turn around she urged him on and he leapt forward, jumping safely to the other side of the canyon.

Even more worried after watching Vicki's attempt, we each crossed in turn, holding our breaths and hoping we'd make it to the other side. As the last hoof landed safely on the cliff on the far side and dust rained down into the crevice below, we looked at each other in relief — too shaken to ride, we led the horses in the direction we hoped would lead back to the trailer. Twenty minutes later, in shallow dips in the rocks, we found pools of water covered in slime; by now our horses were so thirsty that they fought the reins, drinking until no water was left. Mounting again we carried on, slightly envious that the horses had drunk. Soon we began recognising landmarks; we were still about an hour from the trailer but at least we knew which way to go.

A narrow and dirty stream seeped out of the rocks, and still wanting water the horses bent their heads to drink. Half-falling out of the saddles, we dropped to our knees and used our hands to scoop water and drink — more than willing to put up with the stale taste as opposed to waiting to get back to the trailer; desperate times called for desperate measures.

With huge relief we rounded the final bend and saw the trailer. We'd been riding for almost four hours, through the middle of the day; without a doubt it was the worst ride of our trip so far, and we hurriedly unsaddled, wanting to get back on the road and out of Utah as fast as possible. Leaving Jackie to stand, I lifted the saddle up into the trailer; Vicki cried out and I turned to see Jackie and Smith galloping off into the distance. Kirsty vaulted back on Digit and galloped across the plains after them, while I ran behind on foot; already fatigued from our ride, it was the last thing any of us needed. Fortunately, the horses soon stopped, and Kirsty circled around them to slowly approach from behind; within minutes, we had them caught. Jumping on Jackie I rode her back to the trailer while Kirsty led Smith, and we were careful to keep a good hold of the horses' ropes until all seven were safely loaded.

With almost the entire day wasted, and having driven the equivalent of only three hours since leaving the mechanic's, we started off — committed to getting as far as possible before stopping for the night. By late afternoon we had crossed back into Colorado; too tired to drive further and in urgent need of food, we pulled in at the local rodeo grounds. After settling the horses, our first priority was to wash away the sweat and dust, but unable to justify the expense of a hotel room we stopped under a bridge and stripped down to our underwear to wash ourselves in the dirty, flooded river. It was the lowest point in our journey; as cars drove over the bridge and hooted their horns we had to laugh — just to keep from crying. Feeling somewhat cleaner we ate quickly before returning to load the Mustangs; although we'd planned to stay the night, a wind storm had started up and the horses were being pummelled by dust clouds, the fine sand getting in their eyes and driving them crazy.

We drove for a few more hours in the dark, arriving in the town of

Vernal, in north-east Utah, at midnight. Helping ourselves to the yards at the showgrounds, we gave the horses hay and water before setting up our bedding and crashing for the night.

At sunrise we were up again: we still had six more hours of driving and had to meet our guests the following morning. Of course things didn't go to plan — after stopping for gas just before the Wyoming state line we heard the unmistakable hiss of air from a tyre; sure enough, we'd driven over a nail. Naturally, the closest town with a tyre shop was an hour back the way we'd come. Not willing to back-track we continued north to Wyoming, hoping to get to the next town before the tyre was completely flat — a slim chance considering that the truck was pulling a full load. Hopefully we'd at least make it as far as possible, though, so that our call-out fee wouldn't be too high. Within a few minutes, however, the tyre was so flat that the truck was wobbling; defeated, we pulled over. With no phone reception we flagged down the first car to pass and explained our situation — as luck would have it, the guy had his own workshop just a few minutes down the road and offered to repair it for us. Driving slowly, we followed him, and 10 minutes later were back on the road, the tyre bogged and refilled with air.

We finally made it back to Wyoming later that evening, with just hours to spare. We'd been gone for 43 days and had covered 3000 miles (5000 kilometres), and it was good to be back. That night we fell into our own beds, relieved to have survived our road trip with no casualties, and looking forward to meeting our guests the following day.

THE NEXT MORNING, WE WERE UP EARLY to drive the two hours to Jackson. This was one of our favourite towns in America by far, and its Old West charm was both authentic and sophisticated. After meeting our guests, which included two from New Jersey, nine from New Zealand and one from Australia, we spent the afternoon playing tourist: exploring art galleries and photography exhibitions, trying on Western hats and watching a staged stand-off in the town square. The sheriff was riding a Mustang, and we stopped to talk to him and admire his once-wild gelding, who was unfazed by the crowds and the traffic.

From there we went out to dinner before watching the local rodeo. Unlike the Pro Rodeo in Cortez, which had featured animals and athletes at the top of their game, the Jackson Hole Rodeo was more like Bryce Canyon's — an evening of entertainment designed for tourists wanting a Wild West experience. Fortunately, our guests had nothing to compare it with, and they seemed to be a great group.

After a night in Jackson, we headed back to the ranch. The dude ranch had five full days planned for our guests and we would also be riding out with them on our Mustangs, socialising around the campfire and doing a horse-starting demonstration with two young horses. The first was Rayna, who was finally sound after three weeks of having her bandages and dressings changed, and the second was Lacy, a three-year-old ranch horse who would be joining the dude ranch's trekking string in the coming season. It was strange being back at the dude ranch in the middle of the season — no longer was it like an abandoned ghost town, and the yards were full with over 80 horses. Wranglers bustled around matching riders to horses, and soon everyone was mounted and ready to ride.

Unlike the red, barren landscape we'd left behind six weeks earlier, the Wind River valley was now teeming with life. The valley floor was covered in lush green grass, and leaves had returned to the cottonwood trees and created a strong contrast with the rock cliffs that bordered both sides of the property. Elk, mule deer and moose could be found along the river's edge. Each day our guests rode out for hours and we took turns joining them, covering new terrain each day. The horses that stayed behind were schooled in the afternoon, developing their freestyle routines — training sessions that the guests enjoyed watching. All three of the Extreme Mustang Makeover mares had their strengths and weaknesses, and we were able to tailor their routines to suit each horse.

Coyote was now by far the most solid in general; despite her issues in the early days, we were confident that she would produce the best freestyle — so long as she could make it through the compulsory section. She was bold and brave, even confidently working with a tarpaulin as it was waved over her, trotting under it and over it, and jumping it folded

LEFT
Coyote walking calmly
under the tarp as it lifts
up behind her to replicate
the motion of a wave.

BELOW
Jackie and I proudly carrying
the New Zealand flag.

LEFT
Kirsty and Digit demonstrating how quiet she is; Kirsty is standing on her and catching a ball while Digit is bridleless.

BELOW
Bragg trekking out in Shoshone National Forest during our USA Showtym Retreat.

into a jump with people holding each end. She was bold and brave, but unfortunately she was still quite opinionated and made it known if she didn't want to do something; having to do set patterns might prove to be her downfall. Coyote disagreed that side passes and turns on the haunches were a good idea, and would often freeze and refuse to move sideways; both of these were Western manoeuvres that were required as part of the compulsory patterns.

Jackie would do well in the compulsories — her roll-backs, spins, canter to halts, halt to canters, rein-backs and side passes were becoming established and were only going to improve over the next few weeks. Already she was more advanced than any wild horse I'd trained, in half the amount of time. Even her freestyle options were coming along well, although they hadn't really been our focus. She was an honest jumper with a good technique, was happy to have anything carried on her, and, although not as unflappable as Coyote, she was relaxed and more willing than most horses we'd worked with. Whether carrying helium balloons, flags or flying capes, she kept the same steady rhythm, and the one time I rode her bridleless she was responsive and I was able to trust her completely while cantering her around the pasture. I didn't pursue the bridleless work, however, feeling that there wasn't enough time to train her sufficiently when we still had a week's trekking through the Grand Tetons and Yellowstone National Park ahead of us, giving us limited time to work the horses before the competition.

In many ways Digit was at the same stage as Jackie — all of her lateral moves were progressing well, although not quite as established, and they could both do the same freestyle elements. The main difference between the two was the way they responded to things — Jackie was slow and thoughtful, whereas Digit was sharp and responsive — sometimes overthinking or working too quickly through movements, although these characteristics made her better in other areas. Digit's sliding stops were the best of all the horses', as were her transitions and her ability to work bridleless, reacting to the slightest cues and learning how to stop and turn much sooner than the others. She had zero tolerance for the tarpaulin, however, and refused to work within sight of it. Rather than enforcing the issue, we kept it out of sight so that she would remain settled. There was no rule saying that a horse had to be able to cope with abnormal objects; most of our showjumpers wouldn't have coped with it, and it was truly remarkable how tolerant Jackie and Coyote were.

With the mares in training, the prison Mustangs were out on the trails learning to jump. Although they had only jumped twice, once in Delta and once at the Parelli Ranch, the horses hadn't forgotten a thing. Vicki and Amanda would aim the geldings for every fallen tree they could find, and soon they were even jumping over the boundary fences into the Indian reservation to give the horses a bigger challenge. Parker and Smith were very honest and willing, but it was Bragg that was truly special; he cleared everything with plenty of room to spare.

Every evening before dinner, Vicki worked with Lacy and Rayna. Lacy was spoilt and lacked manners, with little respect for people and a short attention span which made it difficult gaining and keeping her focus — something that is crucial when backing a young horse for the first time. Twenty minutes into her first session, however, she relaxed and focused on Vicki, and soon Vicki was sitting astride her, bareback and in a halter like most of the horses she starts. Within 40 minutes, Lacy was walking and trotting around the pasture and Vicki gave her a pat and put her away. Rayna was even easier; after three weeks of handling she was soft, willing and curious about people. Within 20 minutes she was also trotting, and with a massive pat Vicki dismounted and let her loose with the other horses, satisfied with how light and responsive she was.

By the end of the week both horses were cantering under saddle, and on our last ride out with our guests, Vicki took Lacy out on the trails for a four-hour ride. The young mare strode out well and was brave, not putting a foot wrong and slotting into the routine of a trail horse well. She was quite happy to follow and stay in line, but also confident leading — something she would be expected to do for the first few years as one of the horses the wranglers ride, before guests would be allowed on her. Vicki was hugely impressed with the mare, who had come so far in just three days.

During their stay, we also took our guests to Turtle Ranch to watch

Amanda and Bragg jumping the boundary fence into the Shoshone Indian Reservation, a month after he learnt to jump.

Top
Vicki and Rayna during their 'starting' demonstration.

Bottom
Our visit to Turtle Ranch influenced us hugely and watching Robin
work really refined the way we train our own horses.

Robin Wiltshire work with horses and other animals he was training for films. We'd always loved watching the Budweiser commercials, amazed by what the famous Clydesdales could achieve, and when we heard the horses were trained at a ranch just half an hour away, we organised a visit and called in on our way up to Jackson.

We'd been so inspired by Robin's philosophies and training methods that we asked to return a second time with our guests. It was remarkable seeing the improvement in the horses, and also a zebra, after just a few sessions.

Both Robin and his horses have a very relaxed, easy way about them, and seeing the way he worked with them was awe-inspiring for us. While very similar to our own way of training, we learnt so much from watching Robin work, and those two days with him were hugely influential and have greatly improved the way we train our own horses.

On our last evening we had stories and songs around the campfire, and took time reflecting on the week we'd had. Great friendships had been made; it was a week to remember. The next morning, all but three packed and loaded their bags onto the truck; Paige (my American mom, who I'd gotten to know five years earlier during my time with Camp America) and her friend Sarah were staying a few extra days to ride through Yellowstone National Park with us before they flew back to New Jersey, and Tracey (the youngest of our guests and a close family friend) was staying for the rest of our time in America. While our guests said a final goodbye to the wranglers, we drove the trailer to the corrals to load our horses; we'd already said our farewells, since this would also be our last day here.

Riding the Mustangs
with our mums.

CHAPTER 14

Family holiday
— Wilson style

Once in Jackson we headed to the rodeo grounds with our horses, unloading them into stalls before going in search of someone to ask about them staying. It was already late evening, but fortunately the groundskeeper was on-site and offered to let us stay for no cost — saving us hundreds of dollars — on the condition we help him muck out the stalls. This was something we were only too happy to do.

The next day we woke to light rain, and since our trailer was by no means waterproof we pulled our bedding away from the walls and moved it undercover in the rodeo barn — before saddling the horses to make the most of the indoor arena. It was good opportunity to refine what the horses had practised at the dude ranch, and now we were down to final tweaking: working on their consistency, and refining the required manoeuvres.

All three had their stops down perfect, and since we were presenting the horses in English style we would be forgiven for not producing a sliding stop. The turn on the haunches and side passes were Jackie's forté; Digit still got distracted and moved her hind feet or stepped forward, and Coyote stiffened up and rarely got any sideways motion at all. After putting Jackie away I returned to the arena to assist Coyote on the ground, reinforcing Alexa's ridden aids by pushing against the mare's shoulder. It wasn't long before she gained a clearer understanding of what was required, and the mare relaxed, did a few steps to the side, and then went on to complete half a turn on the haunches.

The next day Mum, Kerrin (Alexa's mum) and Frances (a close family friend) arrived early — it was the first time Mum had been to America, and she was excited to see the scenery and our Mustangs. They couldn't have flown into a better part of the country: Jackson, Wyoming, was in the shadow of the Grand Tetons and was a spectacular welcome. After meeting our Mustangs, and watching them train in the arena that afternoon, we took Mum, Kerrin and Frances to Jackson to see the sights before having dinner. As my birthday was approaching, Mum, Vicki and Amanda bought me a stunning set of blue agate bookends with quartz crystals to celebrate my first book, *For the Love of Horses*, hitting number one on the bestsellers list. Early the following morning we headed north to Yellowstone National Park. Although we'd been there months earlier to explore on foot, it would be our first time riding the horses through the vast landscape, and we were excited to ride out among the buffalo.

After some convincing, our mums agreed to ride our once-wild horses; Kerrin hoped on Digit, Mum rode Jackie, Frances rode Parker, and Paige (who'd joined us for the retreat then, at the last minute, decided to stay a few extra days) rode Smith. Amanda was on Bragg, Tracey rode Coyote, and Vicki took Rayna out for her first trail ride. Although initially cautious, the mums were soon relaxing in the saddle and confidently cantering along the trails. It really showed how well-trained the Mustangs had become. Seeing our mums enjoy themselves was priceless, if exhausting — as we were short of horses, Kirsty and I were having to run on foot to keep up and Alexa and Sarah stayed with the truck and trailer.

An hour into the ride we found buffalo in Hayden Valley. These wild animals are prone to charging and we'd been warned of the danger, so we kept well back, skirting around the edges before heading back towards the trailer. The horses were soon unsaddled, and we took them for a swim in the river nearby. Amanda decided that she wanted a shot for the documentary and passed her horse to Mum, while Tracey, Vicki, Kirsty and I cantered along the shallow part of the river for a video. Water was flying around us as we cantered around the bend and approached the camera, and when Jackie pitched slightly I mentally panicked and threw myself off to the side to avoid falling off. With a thud I hit the water and sank beneath the surface; when I emerged, I looked around to see Parker and Jackie cantering riderless alongside the other two girls. With a laugh I saw Tracey emerge from the water beside me — when I'd bailed, it had given Parker a fright and sent Tracey flying.

Sopping wet, we caught our Mustangs and jumped back on for one last swim before loading up and heading north to Montana. On the drive north through the park we saw an abundance of wildlife, including a black bear and her cubs, a seven-point elk and a charming chipmunk that climbed onto our laps to say hello. At every thermal spring we stopped, looking at the bubbling mud pools, painted pots and geysers that Yellowstone is famous for. Our Mustangs waited patiently on the trailer while we explored, and when we finally made it to Mammoth, at the north entrance of Yellowstone, it was getting dark. Since the Mammoth Hot Springs and Canary Springs were our favourites, we decided to return at sunrise, and loaded the horses at dawn the next morning to return to the park. Not long after, we split up: our mums headed south-west in their rental car to see the rest of the thermal highlights, Paige and Sarah left for the airport and we took the horses south-east to ride into the mountains in search of Cache Lake, reputed to be one of the best riding trails in Yellowstone.

After taking yet another wrong turn on the ride, we back-tracked and headed up the right trail, quickly gaining altitude. Wildflowers grew on both sides of the track, and we climbed still higher. Soon we reached a heavily wooded area, and it quickly became apparent that we were in grizzly country — claw marks were gouged into the tree trucks — and we kept a cautious eye out for bears. The trees opened up to a mountain valley, and we cantered along the river banks until we reached the far tree line. Unlike the first two hours, mosquitos attacked us relentlessly as we rode up these higher trails, and although the tracks were narrow and steep we urged the horses on just to escape the onslaught. After 20 minutes we broke from the trees and saw that we'd finally reached the lake, but still there was no relief from the bloodthirsty insects. Stopping only long enough for a photo, we hightailed it off the mountain and made rapid progress through the trees, only letting the Mustangs fall back to a walk once we were past the mosquitos.

Tired and hungry, we returned to the trailer and loaded up, heading east to met our mums in Cody, Wyoming. There was a rodeo on there, and we thought it would be a valuable opportunity to get our horses in an arena with signage and in front of crowds again. Our entries to compete were accepted, although we would be run in the second string at the conclusion of the rodeo; but unlike Bryce Canyon, they imposed a strict dress code — full-length Western shirts had to be worn, and although we'd spent months in the Western-dominated Wild West, we

Top
Amanda and Bragg checking out the bear scratches on a tree trunk.

Bottom
A seven-point elk in Yellowstone National Park.

still hadn't acquired any. With only an hour before the rodeo started, we went around asking other competitors if they had a shirt we could borrow, and finally one of the cowboys quite literally took the shirt off his back and handed it to us — not only to use in the Barrel Race but also to keep as a memento of our time in Cody.

Now looking the part, we headed to the stands to watch the earlier classes before going over to the yards to saddle up in the dark. The horses were relaxed and working well, warming up in a crowded ring — under spotlights — and finally they announced the start of the competition. Jackie was up first but froze in the entrance, worried about walking through the narrow alleyway that led into the arena. Since reassurance wasn't working, Vicki ran down and gave her a pat before walking in front of her. Following tentatively, she entered the arena and trotted just a few metres before she froze again. Wanting the experience to be as productive as possible, I sat quietly, letting her take everything in, and once I felt her relax I picked up the trot again, bending in a pattern around the barrels before cantering slowly across the finish line. We had a lot of work to do before the competition in just two weeks' time! Next in was Digit, who was also worse than we expected, and with just Coyote to go things weren't looking promising. We certainly hadn't entered hoping to win or place, simply riding for the experience, but it was highlighting just how little the horses were prepared for the competition environment of the Extreme Mustang Makeover — they had spent far too much time on the trails, although we wouldn't have changed a thing if we could have done it again.

Coyote then entered the arena, and although we'd been hesitant about entering her at all, she went from a walk to canter and expertly navigated the barrels before cantering over the finish line. When the stands were empty, we asked the organisers if we could run through the barrels again for practice, which they were more than happy to let us do. For the next 20 minutes we took the Mustangs slowly along the fence line, getting them used to the colourful signage before working them again through the barrels; this time they cantered around like pros — the extra time in the arena had been just what they'd needed.

From Cody we headed north, crossing back into Montana. We'd heard of Cloud, the famed wild stallion of the Pryor Mountains, and were hoping to go in search of his herd. Using a roughly drawn map, we followed gravel roads in search of the 120 horses that roamed in the alpine meadows. We didn't anticipate how much altitude we would gain, or how rough the tracks would be, and we were in for a rough trip. Fortunately, we'd unhitched the trailer and left it, along with the horses, at yards near the main road — it would have been impossible to have ridden, or towed anything, up these off-road tracks.

Over rocks we juddered, at times crawling due to the rough terrain; it was going to be a long drive to the top. The landscape was barren desert as far as the eye could see, and we wondered how any horses could survive here, let alone a herd. After an hour of averaging a mere 20 miles (30 kilometres) per hour, the rocky desert gave way to towering forests. Another hour on, we traversed around the head of a canyon and once again drove over rocks. Then the trees and rocks quickly fell behind us, and lush green meadows scattered with wild flowers became the norm; we were now in the area of the Pryor Mountains where the herds roamed, and we kept a sharp eye out for horses.

Twenty minutes later we found our first herd — buckskins that clearly showed their Spanish ancestry. The horses of the Pryor Mountains are most similar in type to those from the Sulphur Mountains, and some of the most genetically pure. Unlike the Sulphur horses, however, this stallion didn't round up his herd and leave as soon as he saw the truck approach, and even when we hopped out he stood with his herd and watched us curiously. They were obviously well used to people; despite the horrendous three-hour drive up the mountain, they must have got their fair share of visitors coming to see the most widely known wild herds in America, made famous by the palomino stallion Cloud whose life had been documented many times since his birth was caught on camera by a film-maker 20 years earlier.

Hoping to find Cloud, we left the herd of buckskins and headed left down a side track, which soon became impassable. Disheartened, we went back the way we had come and turned left at the fork instead of

Top
A wild Mustang mare approaches Vicki at sunset in the Pryor Mountains.

Bottom
A wild Mustang foal sleeps among the wild flowers.

right. Within minutes, we saw a herd of horses on a hill in the distance. Parking the truck, we climbed out, grabbing our cameras and heading out on foot.

A short way along we found a lone palomino filly with a young buckskin colt; both had been rolling in red dust and looked pink in the evening light. After watching them for a while we continued on to where we'd seen the larger herd, and as we crested the hill we were mesmerised. Over 100 horses grazed in the valley, and not wanting to disturb them we settled down to watch. Stallions fought playfully — young bachelors vying for attention, and old battle-scarred warriors warning others away from their herds. Foals frolicked in the wild flowers and mares grazed nearby. It was the circle of life in its entirety, so rarely seen. And complete with Cloud himself, the aged stallion, grazing on his own at the head of the valley; too old to have a herd of his own, but still within range of the other horses for company, quietly keeping to himself to avoid conflict.

Circling behind the horses, we headed for the tree line to sit and watch the herds from a closer distance without scaring them off — this was their home, and we were only too happy to be mere observers. Amanda set herself up in a dried-up river bed, quietly filming the horses interacting. Although we were off to the side, we drew the horses' attention; but rather than fleeing they inched closer, curious about these two-legged creatures in their domain. Soon herds stood on every side, with more coming through the trees towards us. Some stopped 100 metres back and quickly grew bored, settling down to graze, but the younger ones kept coming closer. One young filly boldly stepped within 2 metres of Vicki and lowered her head curiously. Talking quietly, Vicki remained still until the filly's courage failed her and she stepped back and trotted back to her herd.

We had been so absorbed by the buckskin filly that we hadn't even noticed a young foal creeping closer; when we turned, it was a shock to find the little black foal far from its mother's side, intent on Amanda. With the camera raised she filmed the foal's approach, until it stopped within a metre of her. Keeping her hands steady, Amanda captured the foal's indecision on film, including the subtle shift in its facial expression

Top
A Mustang foal approaches Amanda as she films the wild herds in the Pryor Mountains.

Bottom
An older wild stallion rests under the trees.

as it decided that Amanda wasn't a threat. In the distance the mare and stallion watched, not concerned enough to interfere but ready to move if necessary. Boldly, the black foal stepped forward and stretched out its tiny muzzle, nudging the camera before quickly retreating. It then stepped even closer, lowering its face to the camera again, and Amanda raised her hand to protect the lens from being damaged. To her surprise, the movement didn't worry the foal; instead, — it lowered its head curiously and nudged her hand, making contact with a human for the first time. Knowing that it's not a good idea to interact with wild herds, Amanda dropped her hand and slowly withdrew, and the foal quickly lost interest and returned to its mother. Amanda could hardly believe what had just happened.

Sunset was now fast approaching. We walked around the herds, capturing photos of the iconic horses, especially amazed by the grullos and roans — two colours we'd rarely seen in the captive Mustangs in the BLM yards. During the two hours we spent with the herds that evening we saw over a dozen stallion fights; most playful, others with more serious intent. It was intriguing that so many horses were gathered in the same valley when there were 94,000 acres (38,000 hectares) for them to roam over and plenty of grass to be found; in the Kaimanawa Ranges the herds all stay separate, and only gather in the Argo Valley in the winter to get below the snow line.

With darkness setting in, we hiked back to the truck and found a place to camp for the night; we'd brought blankets and a tarpaulin up with us and were planning to sleep under the stars. Finding a nice grove of trees, we set up camp — even dinner was civilised, as we'd brought the food needed to make burritos. As night fell we settled on the tarp, bundled in clothes and blankets and wondering why on earth we hadn't brought more clothes; it was freezing on top of the mountain. With two layers of jeans, gloves, a beanie, two jackets and double layers of socks, I did manage to sleep; everyone else had half the amount of clothing and had restless nights trying to stay warm. Since most of us were awake at sunrise, we took the truck out to try to find the herds before the sun rose over the horizon. The valley where they'd been the night before was empty; they obviously only migrated there in the evenings to drink at the water hole. Finally we found about 40 of them by a thicket of trees and captured photos of foals sleeping in the wild flowers and, again, stallions fighting. This time, though, we watched an older stallion fight with a young colt from his herd, almost as if he was training him for future battles — he was always careful not to hurt the colt and, although they reared and struck out, their antics lacked malice or power.

The moment we got the truck moving on our way back there was a clunking noise. We looked under the truck, at the tyres and at the engine, but since we were all naïve when it came to trucks we weren't quite sure what to look for. All we knew was that something was significantly wrong, we were on top of a mountain with a hell of a drive ahead of us and there was no cell-phone reception. As hiking down the mountain to find a mechanic wasn't an option, we decided to start driving and pray that we'd make it; we thought we might have done something to damage the truck's four-wheel-drive and we hoped it wouldn't worsen by driving on it.

After clunking halfway down the mountain at a crawling pace, we stopped at a signpost to explore some ice caves. Although it was summer, with no snow in sight, the caves were so cold that they stayed solid ice with amazing ice formations in the centre of the cavern. From there we drove past the forest, where we saw a brown bear in the trees, then bumped back over the rocky tracks, wincing at the noise the truck was making. As soon as we reached the bottom of the mountain we called a mechanic, but rather than driving out to have a look they told us to drive the truck into the shop — we'd already driven three hours on it at this point, and a little further wouldn't kill it. Like we'd suspected, the four-wheel-drive was stuffed and would cost US$1700 to repair; even worse, it would take a week to fix. The competition, 10 hours' drive south-east, was now only 10 days away. Instead, they manually forced the truck back into two-wheel-drive and said we'd be fine to tow the horses back to Idaho before fixing it. After a quick phone call to the dealers we'd bought it from, they said we could drop it off broken and they'd just take the repair cost off the buy-back price. Relieved that we wouldn't have to worry about it further, we loaded the horses on the trailer and headed south. In hindsight the trip up the mountain side had been an expensive one, but it had also been a highlight of our time in America — nothing could overshadow how special those memories were.

WE BACK-TRACKED TO CODY THAT NIGHT, planning to stay at the rodeo grounds so that the horses could have one last practice in the arena. But gale-force winds whipped up a storm, and barely able to stand ourselves we decided it wasn't fair to keep the horses yarded there overnight. We stopped just long enough to shower, keeping the Mustangs on the trailer, and were soon back on the road . . . this time with no end destination in sight and only an hour to go before nightfall. Just before the Yellowstone park entrance, however, we found public yards beside a swollen river and unloaded and set up camp for the night. Signs surrounding the yards warned people to beware of grizzly bears in the area and we yarded the Mustangs strategically: none of the horses were alone, so they were less vulnerable, and we kept them in the yards closest to the trailer in case we needed to help them in the middle of the night. Next we sought to keep ourselves protected, making sure any food was off the ground and covered, before falling asleep — we were getting plenty of early nights with our rustic camping, since we had no light for doing anything after dark.

The next morning, we woke early and drove through Yellowstone and on to Grand Teton National Park. A guy we'd met at the public yards had recommended two of his favourite rides. The first was to Jenny Lake, with several crossings over narrow bridges, and the second was up through Paintbrush Canyon, climbing in altitude until you reached the divide almost 10,000 feet (3000 metres) above sea level. Deciding to tackle the easier trail first, we rode out on the Mustangs, once again letting our mums ride. The experience and the scenery were too spectacular for them to miss out on, and we gave them Jackie, Smith and Parker. Tracey doubled behind Alexa on Coyote, leaving just one person to hike out on foot.

Kirsty was a champ, and offered to walk so that I could ride and

Alexa and Tracey doubling on Coyote in the Grand Teton National Park.

photograph from Digit; soon we were off, quickly coming across the first narrow footbridge — with no sides — that spanned the rapids below. The horses were hesitant, and rightly so, but once the first horse had crossed the rest gamely followed. From there we followed the lake edge, crossing another long footbridge onto an island before realising we were at a dead end and turning back. At the fork in the path we turned right instead of heading back to the trailer; we were having way too much fun to go back now. We trotted up a few hills while Kirsty ran ahead, and at the top we had an incredible view over two lakes — the one we had just ridden around, and another far below that we were heading to. Again Kirsty took the lead while the Mustangs carefully made their way down the stony steps until the path flattened off again.

Amanda and Kirsty were joking about how terrified they would be if they came across a bear; we all laughed — we'd been in America for almost three months now, and although we'd seen two grizzlies and a brown bear it had never been while riding, so it seemed unlikely. The two of them moved ahead while the rest of us continued walking to give the others, who were still navigating the hill, a chance to catch up. Suddenly we heard a high-pitched scream, which, rather than stopping, became more panicked. Kicking our horses into a canter, we headed down the trail and rounded a corner to see Kirsty sprinting towards us with a panicked look on her face, Amanda cantering behind on Bragg. In a breathless panic, they told us they'd rounded the corner and met a black bear on the path just metres in front of them.

At first they'd frozen, unable to believe what they were seeing, especially after all the joking just moments before. Then the bear had stood on up its hind legs, walking towards them waving its paws, and Kirsty had spun around, grabbed Bragg's reins and begged Amanda to let her climb on the horse with her. Worried that Bragg would panic with two riders and buck them both off, Amanda had refused, instead backing Bragg up and yelling at Kirsty to make a run for it while she kept the agitated horse between the advancing bear and the fleeing girl. Tripping over her feet, Kirsty bolted down the path; once she was sure Kirsty had enough of a head start, Amanda spun Bragg around and quickly followed.

We sat open-mouthed as they recounted their story, and then rode past them in the hope of finding the bear — to see whether they were telling the truth or just joking around. Sure enough the bear was still there, although it had wandered a short way off the path, crossed a shallow creek and now stood watching us from the trees. It was only a tiny thing, too — nothing like the grizzlies we'd seen — and it looked young; not nearly as menacing as they had made it sound. We walked our horses into the creek to get a closer look and noticed that the bear was tagged. It obviously decided we were no longer interesting and wandered away. Alexa and Tracey decided to follow on Coyote, and Amanda and I dismounted and joined them — staying a respectful distance behind but keeping the bear within sight. Coyote was the most interested — she had her ears pricked and a spring in her step, and she followed in the bear's paw prints in a similar fashion to how she'd instinctively followed the cattle at the Parelli Ranch.

Filled with adrenaline, we buzzed for the rest of the ride; when a snake slithered across the path under Smith's legs it barely seemed noteworthy. The Grand Tetons were proving to be a spectacular place to ride, with an abundance of wildlife, and we couldn't wait to ride up to the snow line the next day.

After another quiet night back at the Jackson rodeo grounds, we returned to the Grand Tetons raring to go. Kirsty stayed behind to catch up on sleep after her exhausting encounter with the bear, and the rest of us headed out at sunrise; it was going to be a long ride to the top. We started at 4000 feet (1200 metres) above sea level, rounding a lake before heading up the mountain path and climbing steadily in altitude for the next four hours. We passed through wooded valleys, over raging rivers and along narrow and stony switchbacks. Although horses were allowed on the trail, there were times when we wondered just what we were getting ourselves into, and on a couple of occasions we considered turning the horses around and finishing early.

In places the track was washed out and we had to drop the Mustangs off steep banks to scramble across dry river beds, and further along we had to bash through foliage to circle fallen trees that blocked the path.

Top
Riding with our mums
in the Paintbrush
Canyon in the Grand
Teton National Park.

Middle
Crossing a narrow bridge
on the Mustangs.

Bottom
Snow level near the
Grand Teton divide.

Our horses were brave, and were willing and happy to attempt anything asked of them. The higher we rose, the more breathtaking the scenery became; the park's array of lakes, seen from on top of the mountains, was a spectacular sight. Soon we reached the snow line, and although it was mid-summer there was plenty to be found. Rivers ran under tunnels that had been carved through the ice, and the Mustangs pawed at the snow playfully. We were in the heart of the mountains and sheer rocks surrounded us on every side.

We'd been told to ride to the Grand Teton divide; from there we could continue down another canyon instead of back-tracking down the Paintbrush. But the further we climbed the more cautious we became, and when we met a guide who told us it was too dangerous for the horses to continue, we stopped. Ahead, the shale rocks would be unstable beneath the horses' feet, and in some places snow obscured the path and avalanches had caused the track to disappear completely. Not wanting to risk injuring the horses, we turned back. It had been one of our favourite rides so far, and although we were close to the summit we were actually relieved to be heading back — it was better to be safe than sorry.

The ride down was even more fun, with Alexa and Tracey fooling around on Coyote and keeping us in hysterics with their antics. Tracey would spin around to sit backwards so she could have a conversation with the rider behind, and when the scenery was at its most beautiful she would stand, balancing behind Alexa so that she could enjoy the views. Coyote, who had originally been the most difficult, was by now the most bomb-proof and the girls could do anything on her. It reminded us of the quiet and versatile ponies we'd had as little children — and was hugely impressive for a wild and headstrong mare with fewer than 50 rides since her wild days.

Jackie was all the mums' preferred horse — in fact, she was top of their list of any horse they'd ever ridden. She was sure-footed, steady but not lazy, and was confident either leading at the front or following patiently at the back. She didn't spook or pull on the reins, and she never jig-jogged. And, most importantly, especially for nervous riders, she was light and responsive to the aids. Long before you touched the reins, she would respond to the shift in body weight. People felt safe on her; as we scaled the mountain our mums often swapped onto her so that they could all have a turn on their favourite Mustang. I would then ride Parker or Smith; while also great horses, there was no doubt that the prison geldings weren't as soft as the horses we'd trained from scratch.

After seven hours we reached the trailer, and since it was a hot day and we had no water to wash the horses off, we jumped on them bareback and headed down to the lake to swim them. Since it was a weekend there were people, kayaks and paddle-boards everywhere, but the horses didn't falter, enjoying the cool water and swimming out of their depth while we laughed and had a great time. Between Yellowstone, Pryor Mountains and the Grand Tetons, this had been one of the best weeks of our lives and the perfect finish to our road trip.

Jackie and I during our final practice before the Extreme Mustang Makeover.

CHAPTER 15

Final preparations

As we piled back into the truck and started the long drive to Emmett, Idaho — our base for the last week before the competition — we felt nostalgic; our time in America was coming to an end and it would be so hard to leave our Mustangs behind.

To break up the drive, we called in to stay with one of our fellow trainers, Josh, who had invited us to visit with his family. It was a perfect halfway point, and the horses enjoyed being turned out into pasture overnight while we had the luxury of sleeping in beds.

Josh wasn't what we were expecting, and we loved him for it. He wasn't a big-name trainer out to compete for prize money, prestige, or to raise awareness about the breed. He was simply a man who loved horses, who'd lost his horse a year earlier and who hoped that the Extreme Mustang Makeover process would pair him up with his next forever horse — a Mustang that would become a valued part of the family. Many of his methods were founded on what he'd learnt years earlier by observing the relationship between troubled youth and horses, and more recently from working with adult offenders. He'd found that the body language of troubled humans was very similar to that of a wild horse needing to develop trust.

From the first moment we saw Josh working with Liberty, it was obvious that a forever horse was exactly what he'd found. Like Jackie and me, Kirsty and Digit, Alexa and Coyote, Amanda, Deacon and Bragg, and Vicki with Rayna and Gunnar, his Mustang had become more than just a horse. As we listened to Josh talk, I was envious that he lived in America and had a chance of keeping his Mustang; for sure, if I didn't live on the other side of the world Jackie would remain with me. I hoped Josh would be able to buy Liberty back at auction like he had planned; she couldn't have had a better home.

The next morning we rode out on BLM land with Josh and his wife, Melanie, and as we watched his little bay Mustang we couldn't help but smile. Liberty had convinced Josh of the worth of Mustangs; teaching him as much, if not more, than he'd taught her. The Mustangs had won themselves an advocate for life, and we encouraged Josh to take more Mustangs out and train them through the TIP program, explaining to him how it worked. Feeling like we'd made valued friends, we waved goodbye, looking forward to catching up with them again in just a week's time at the competition.

HAVING ALSO MADE SUCH GOOD FRIENDS WITH JEN, the equine dentist, we were looking forward to spending our final week in America with her. Her property was well set up for our final preparations, with covered yards, paddocks and an arena filled with jumps. Even better it was just 20 minutes from Nampa, where the Extreme Mustang Makeover was to be held, and within driving distance of large towns where we could buy our final outfits and anything needed as props.

While the competition is first and foremost about the welfare of the horses, and producing a soft, well-trained horse is the focus, the judging in the freestyle final is weighted heavily on the 'wow' factor. Music, costumes and crowd-pleasing performances are a must if you want to place well, and although the theatrics certainly weren't a priority for us, it was fun deciding on a theme for each horse and choosing lyrics and an outfit to complement the horse's routine. Kirsty had decided to dress up as Zorro, I was keeping it simple and cultural with a focus on the silver fern — quite suitable as Jackie was solid black — and Alexa had decided on a pirate theme.

It was risky training horses for the freestyle element, and it wasn't our focus in that final week. Our aim earlier on had been to develop each horse's individual strengths, and now it was to focus on the required manoeuvres. Thirty-eight horses had started the competition, and only 10 would make it through to the freestyle finals. The remaining horses that showed up to compete would only be required to do the preliminary classes, which were challenging enough in their own right. The horses had to be caught without a halter, and needed to walk and trot on the lead, load on a trailer, pick up all four hooves, walk, trot and canter, gallop to a halt, halt to a canter, turn on their haunches, rein-back, side pass, open a gate and walk over an obstacle. Although our horses had been doing these moves for some time now, in our last week it was crucial that we refine the basics rather than working on freestyle elements — there

Top
Jackie working on a soft contact during a lesson.

Bottom
Amanda jumping Bragg 4 feet (1.2 metres) during their last ride together in America.

was no point in teaching the horses complicated moves for their freestyle if they didn't have the necessary skills required to qualify in the top 10 anyway.

On our first day at Jen's, we ran the horses through the workout patterns from the 2014 EMM — we'd watched these online and learnt them so that we could train the horses specifically for whatever they might be asked on the day. That first practice highlighted which areas we needed to work on for each horse. Digit had improved dramatically and was now the most straightforward; she was working at the highest level of training, and we were confident that she would qualify in the top 10. Likewise, Jackie had a good chance, although it was impossible to know for sure without seeing how good the other horses were. We felt that both Jackie and Digit were physically and mentally prepared for the challenge, and were schooling so softly that they would be favourites at the event.

Coyote, however, was still a question mark. Although we felt she was the most likely of our three to win the freestyle, we weren't confident she would make it into the top 10. Because to her difficult start she was significantly behind in her training; although in many ways she was the easiest, she still wasn't good at always doing what she was told, when she was told. The Pattern and Trail classes required the horses to do things in a specific order and in a set time-frame — something Coyote was improving with day by day, but with the added pressure of a competition environment we were unsure just how she would cope.

Later that afternoon Vicki and Amanda had their last rides on Rayna and the prison geldings. Bragg, especially, had come to mean a lot to Amanda, and she rode him down to the arena for one last jumping session. Although it was only his fifth time jumping, as always he was brave, bold and honest, jumping around uprights and oxers to 4 feet (1.2 metres) — not bad for a five-year-old Mustang who'd only been ridden for the first time four months previously.

The Mustangs were then loaded onto the trailer to be delivered to a family we'd met during our travels. They were adopting Deacon and had agreed to graze our other Mustangs for us since we were required to maintain ownership of the prison horses for 12 months. Rachel, the mother, had worked for years as a veterinary assistant and was experienced in working with wild Mustangs, so was perfectly qualified to take care of them; the family also had plenty of pasture for them to roam over, and lots of hay to supplement them over the winter snowstorms. Even better, Rachel was capable of treating minor injuries and experienced enough to catch and handle recently wild horses, even if left untouched for months, if they needed their hooves done or had to be moved.

Returning in the early hours of the morning, at sunrise Vicki struggled out of bed to give us a lesson. As Digit had worked through the basics with such precision and in such a relaxed manner the day before, Vicki asked Kirsty to run through her freestyle routine just once. We'd chosen music and choreographed the routines, and it was a good opportunity to check that the timing was working. A significant part of Digit's routine was to be done bridleless, and she was coming along well — she was now as accurate with no gear on as she was with a halter or bridle. Digit was also confident working with the Zorro cape, but apart from these additions the workout essentially incorporated the same moves from the compulsories — better to do something well than confuse the horses by teaching them too many new things. With four days still left to practise Kirsty was feeling confident, and rightly so — she'd produced a beautiful, well-rounded mare and could now enjoy some fun last rides; their routines had been perfected, and they would run through it once more before the competition just to make sure they were on form.

On their second practices, both Jackie and Coyote also performed well. It was Jackie's second time with helium balloons dancing on a flowing cape behind her, and she couldn't have cared less. Likewise, working with a flag, jumping, leg-yielding, flying changes, and working on a soft and consistent contact was child's play to her, and her gallop to halt was so accurate that I barely stayed on her in my English saddle. We uploaded a video of Jackie working to YouTube, and had plenty of interest in her — she was rumoured to be the favourite going into the competition and people were driving from as far as the West Coast to bid on her at auction. The variety of interested people ranged from Western

Top
Bragg and Rayna turned out to pasture.

Bottom
Kirsty's last ride on Digit before she went lame, working bridleless and bareback.

riders right through to a jumping rider wanting a Mustang as a mascot for their stables.

Coyote was equally impressive on our second run-through, working well through the basics, and although she wasn't asked to work on a contact she was kind and naturally well-rounded. Happy that the basics were good enough, Alexa ran her through her freestyle once — and yet again we were wowed. Never, at any level of training, had we had a horse — especially an ex-wild one — that was just so unfazed and relaxed about anything and everything asked of it. It was even more impressive since we had been there for her entire journey and knew first-hand just how far she'd come from those early days. Alexa had perfected a move we'd named The Wave, a complicated routine where a large tarpaulin was lifted up behind Coyote as she trotted over it, eventually flying above her as she continued trotting on a loose rein under the billowing mass. Designed to resemble a wave, to match Alexa's pirate theme, we were disheartened to then learn that no one was allowed in the arena with a competitor and therefore it wouldn't be possible to recreate it, nor the doubling she had hoped to do with Tracey, like they'd done in the Grand Tetons. Alexa had to adapt her routine to canter in holding the flying tarp in one hand, before halting, dismounting, covering the mare with the tarp and then mounting under it and riding off.

While not as impressive to watch, fortunately it showcased Coyote's remarkable nature to the same extent and was a good compromise. Combined with dropping an anchor and doing a sliding stop within range of the rope, and riding the mare facing backwards, it would be a crowd-pleasing performance and really demonstrate just how versatile and safe the mare had become — invaluable in terms of potential buyers. Coyote was slowly gaining her own fan base; the story of our journey, readily available through social media and updated almost daily since we'd collected the Mustangs, had allowed people to see just what the horses had done and to get a feel for their personalities and quirks.

The next morning we woke early to take the horses for a trail ride. Summer in Idaho was almost unbearable and we were struggling in the heat, preferring to ride either before eight in the morning or after eight at night. Kirsty clipped a rope on Digit and went to lead her in, but it was immediately obvious that she was lame. Leading her slowly to the tie-up area, Kirsty checked over her hooves and legs but nothing appeared sore. Concerned, she ran cold water on Digit's legs before putting her away, hoping that the mysterious lameness would resolve itself within 24 hours; otherwise we'd take her to the vet. Coyote and Jackie enjoyed their lazy trail ride along the canal and we had a relaxing time meandering along the water's edge. After letting them lose in the pasture we headed inside to finalise our costumes and start packing; all three of us also had some last-minute planning to do, not only for the competition but also in preparation to leave. The day after we competed we were flying to Hawaii, then on to Alaska and Canada for a month's holiday, and we had a lot to organise — we also wanted the last days with our horses to be as stress-free as possible so that we could enjoy our time with them.

Wanting a fun last ride before the challenge, we took the horses to Black Canyon Dam for a swim on the Thursday morning, on the way to Nampa. It had been exactly 100 days since we first got our horses, and the day was filled with lots of laughter and good times; playing in the water, swimming and fooling around. It was a time for just us and our mares, celebrating how far we'd come in the best way we knew how; a day to remember. As I sat on Jackie in the river, I was hit by the reality of leaving her behind in just a few days' time, and felt compelled to act. As soon as the time zones allowed, I called New Zealand and talked with potential sponsors to work out the logistics of flying a horse home from America. It would be a costly exercise, although they were willing to help fund part of it. I was torn — there was a chance she would find a great home anyway, although with the auction system it was impossible to know who was bidding, and the cost of purchasing her as well as flying her home would be excessive. I would have to bid against the public for her at auction, and as one of the most well-known horses competing she was guaranteed to fetch a good price.

My hopes were dashed when the Mustang Heritage Foundation and the BLM explained that even if I bought her, I'd have to have title of

Top
Our last swim on the Mustangs, 100 days after we first started our journey together.

Bottom
Alexa and Coyote at sunset on the evening before we left for the Extreme Mustang Makeover.

her for a full year before she could be exported overseas — so on top of everything else I would have to pay for her to be grazed in America for a year. It was just so hard to decide. Of any horse that I'd ever owned, at any point in my life, she was my number one; but realistically, she was a 14.3-hand Mustang who wouldn't have much use in New Zealand except as a pleasure or demonstration horse, due to her size. It was my heart saying yes and my head saying a very definite no.

As we pulled up to the Nampa gates, reality hit us: our journey with these horses was most likely ending this weekend, and we had a mere two days to showcase just how special they were, in the hope that not only would they be good ambassadors for the breed, but also to increase their chances of finding good-quality homes.

CHAPTER 16

Extreme Mustang Makeover

Alexa and Coyote during
their freestyle final.

After arriving at the showgrounds, we settled Jackie and Coyote in their stalls and led Digit over to the vet clinic which bordered the Horse Park. Although she had improved a little, she was still noticeably lame at the trot and this would only worsen with work. The vets agreed that she was in no condition to compete, and wrote a vet report so that she could be withdrawn. It was disappointing for Kirsty for sure, but she was also partly relieved. The competition had never been her focus, and regardless of these final few days she would have great memories of her little black Mustang. Digit would be remembered not for how she went for a few minutes in the arena, but for the relationship and adventures they had shared over several months.

Fortunately, a lovely lady that we'd met along our travels had been showing interest in Digit for weeks and had met the mare a number of times. She was prepared to adopt her regardless of whether she was able to compete, so there was no stress about finding a good home for the mare before we flew out in just four days' time. It took a huge burden off Kirsty's shoulders — not knowing who might bid on our horses at auction was one of our biggest worries. Although well-adjusted, our Mustangs were still wild horses with only 100 days of handling and about 60 rides on them. Appearing quiet in the ring didn't mean that they were suited to the level of riders looking for horses, or to the purposes they were wanting to use the horses for. We'd seen first-hand at the auction in Nevada the range of unsuitable people who purchased these horses, and we dreaded someone like that taking them home. It was one of the many reasons I was still considering bidding on Jackie.

Vet report in hand, we went in search of the BLM officials to withdraw Digit from the competition. We had already warned them about her lameness over the phone, and just needed to make it official. To our shock, the BLM insisted that Digit compete despite the vet report, even if it was just in the halter class, so that she could be auctioned off on the final night. Horrified, we argued that not only was this unethical, but nor was it fair on the horse. By presenting a horse in the halter class only, many would wonder whether she had riding or soundness issues; and even those who had followed her progress would question whether her lameness was permanent, greatly reducing how much they would bid for her on auction. While the money didn't matter to us, we were aware that Mustangs are often considered a cheap option for people unable to afford other breeds, and we didn't want Digit to end up in a home where her needs weren't sufficiently met due to a lack of either the money or the experience needed to continue her education.

Even when we explained that we had someone willing to adopt her, the BLM weren't ready to be persuaded. Kirsty was in tears, bitterly upset not only about Digit but about being asked to compromise our integrity and morals regarding horse welfare. It took much convincing before the BLM agreed that Digit could be withdrawn from the Extreme Mustang Makeover and transferred to the TIP program so that she could be adopted privately, and Digit was led away to be stabled and rested.

With now only two of our original five horses in the competition, we had plenty of time and support for preparing the horses. Of the 38 horses assigned to trainers 100 days ago, only 24 were competing this weekend. Like Spring and Red, some had been withdrawn early due to permanent soundness issues; others had been too difficult to tame or had been re-homed by people lacking the experience needed to domesticate them; and still others, like Digit, had been training well but had a minor injury which meant they couldn't compete on the day. Walking down the barn aisles and meeting the other trainers and their horses was very interesting; some were professional trainers doing it to raise their profiles and increase their client bases, others (like us) to raise awareness about the plight of the Mustangs and promote re-homing from the BLM yards, and a few, like Josh, to find their next forever horse.

Watching the horses work in the warm-up ring was also interesting. Some had obviously been trained extensively and specifically to compete, and were well drilled — they knew their jobs, and that was about it. The majority of these horses wouldn't have been ridden bareback, or out on the trails; in fact, several had never left the confines of yards or the arena over the past 100 days. One mare was significantly lame — worse than Digit — but when someone pointed it out the trainer shrugged and said that after two hours of being ridden she always worked out of it.

Another horse had a significantly swollen hock and really shouldn't have been competing, or be offered for auction without a disclaimer. It made us fully aware of the importance of having a vet on-site — at the Kaimanawa Stallion Challenges in New Zealand, all of the horses had to pass a trot-up to ensure that they were sound enough to compete; something that the Mustangs would have benefited from.

That evening we had one last practice in the indoor arena and it was invaluable; allowing the horses to get used to the signage and the grandstands. Coyote was totally relaxed, but Jackie was a little tenser than normal, shying away from the banners that lined the edges. Fortunately, she soon settled and worked softly.

The taming of the wild horses and the adventures we'd had along the way were by far our favourite part, and the upcoming competition was the part we enjoyed the least. It didn't seem right that hundreds of hours' work should be judged by just four minutes in the arena, in the most unfamiliar of circumstances. The next morning, as we saddled our horses for the Pattern class, Alexa and I were half-dreading it — not because the horses weren't capable of doing everything we asked of them, because they were, but because it so rarely goes right on the day, and we didn't want to let our horses down or showcase them poorly. In our eyes Jackie and Coyote were remarkable, and we really wanted people to appreciate and see how special they were, not only for themselves but also for the Mustang breed in general.

The first horses entered the arena, and the variety in their training and the way they worked was evident. Jackie and Coyote were the only horses shown English, with the rest having been trained Western. We felt quite out of place, and the pattern was obviously targeted at Western riders. We'd expected there to be a Western bias in the moves required, but there was little room for translating a lope and pivot — one of the requirements — into English. Fortunately we had been training the horses specifically in these areas. Apart from Jackie striking off on the wrong lead and then doing a flying change to the correct one, both horses did well, finishing with Coyote a respectable seventh and Jackie ninth.

The next class was Handling and Conditioning. When the horses were

IDAHO HORSE PARK

Alexa and Coyote and Jackie and I groomed and ready for our Handling and Conditioning class.

JIM SCHULER PLAZA

let loose in the round pen, Coyote was so relaxed that she walked to the centre, dropped to her knees and rolled. Jackie was also sweet, watching and waiting for me through the rails, and both approached to be caught when the time was up and we were allowed to re-enter the arena. From there our horses trotted smartly beside us before halting, and in the grooming section we crawled between their legs to change sides so we could finish brushing them. Picking up their feet was next. Coyote stood like a rock while Alexa circled her, picking up each hoof, but when it was Jackie's turn she walked off halfway through and I had to return to her head and ask her to halt before I picked up her hind legs. Not surprisingly, after months of road-tripping both horses loaded without hesitation on to the waiting trailer, the last requirement of the workout. To our delight, Alexa placed second and I finished third, putting us comfortably in the top 10 going into the final class the following day.

That night we stayed up late, enjoying a barbeque with the other trainers before returning to the trailer to finalise things for the final day of competition. By midnight I had just fallen asleep when I was awakened by my phone ringing. Groggily I reached for it and said hello. The caller identified himself as Mark, and went on to say that he was interested in Jackie and wanted more information before the auction the following day. Struggling to form a coherent thought, I wondered why he had called so late, but soon enough I understood why: Mark was an advisor to the Special Forces, currently based in Iraq on active duty. He went on to say that he was retiring from the military in November and was wanting to spend the next 20 years riding with his wife through the mountains near his home in Northern Idaho.

Wondering how he'd heard about Jackie, I asked whether he'd been following her journey on social media, and he said that his security clearance was so high he didn't have Facebook. Rather, he'd been giving a lecture to some New Zealand soldiers and afterwards they talked about their plans on returning home. Mark mentioned that he'd been looking for the right Mustang for years, and wanted to ride through forests, National Parks and wilderness areas on a once-wild horse. The Kiwis had perked up, telling Mark about how wild horses roam in the Waiouru

Top
Our fan club included our mums and many of the Americans we had met during our travels.

Bottom
Jackie trotting out during the Handling and Conditioning class where we placed third.

Military Training Ground in their home country, then went on to talk about the three sisters who had dedicated so much of their time to saving them from slaughter and training them.

To show Mark, they pulled up videos on YouTube and stumbled across the latest one we'd uploaded of Jackie — who was everything he'd been looking for in a Mustang. The information beneath the video included contact details, and now here we were talking at length about my special mare. Once Mark's questions were answered, I set about interviewing him to find out how much experience he had, what sort of home he could offer, and his philosophy on horsemanship and preferred training methods; everything he said sounded ideal. For the first time I wasn't dreading the approaching auction — I had real hopes that he'd follow through and bid on her. By now it was two in the morning, and I sent Mark a quick email with more information, videos and photos so that he knew as much about Jackie as possible. Fortunately he was well aware of the EMM process, having attended as many auctions as he could over the past five years in search of his dream horse, and also knew what to expect from a 100-day Mustang.

The next morning I woke dazed; I recounted the phone call I'd had with the others, it sounded too good to be true. But it really had happened, and by 9 a.m. Mark was on the phone to the Extreme Mustang Makeover and BLM officials to sort through the logistics of silent bidding, transporting options and clearing US$10,000 (NZ$15,000) on his credit card in case the bidding went that high. It really was happening, and it was fortunate that I loved the sound of the home Mark could offer because most assuredly, with a silent bid of five figures to beat, I could no longer afford to buy her at auction even if I'd wanted to.

FOLLOWING A LARGELY SLEEPLESS NIGHT AND WITH too much to think about, I disappeared into Jackie's stable for some quiet time before the last class. The Trail class was, by far, what our horses were most suited to; having been out on so many adventures they were used to going just about anywhere and doing just about anything. Alexa was first to go and performed well, although Coyote was a little stiff in her rein-back between the poles laid out on the ground. Sure that Jackie would do well I walked into the ring with high expectations, but these were quickly shattered. From the first walk to canter she was hesitant, and as we trotted through the cones she backed off, spooking at a person sitting in the arena against the fence, waiting there to reposition the poles or cones if a horse knocked them over. The next element of the Trail class was rein-backing through offset poles, and Jackie remained distracted, although I halted her and gave her plenty of time, trying to reassure her. Although she did everything asked of her, she certainly wasn't as relaxed as she could have been, and was unsettled over everything she had practised flawlessly before.

Alexa again did well, finishing third, with me well out of the placings. The top 10 rankings were soon announced, with Alexa placing fourth overall and winning the Young Gun Buckle for the highest-placed trainer under 21. Coyote had been consistent across each of the preliminary classes and was a strong contender going into the final — especially considering that the freestyle would showcase her strengths in a way that was impossible with set patterns. To my surprise and delight, Jackie qualified tenth overall. Although she'd been well up the day before, her poor scoring in the Trail meant that she was the horse with the lowest points to qualify. Fortunately, that wouldn't count against her as each of the top 10 started the finals night with a score of zero.

The top 10 horses were required to complete a 90-second compulsory pattern of advanced Western moves, followed by a four-minute freestyle. I'd almost been relieved when I'd thought Jackie hadn't qualified, due to how exhausting the competition environment had been for the horses. Now that she was back in, I knew it would take every bit of willpower and reserves to get both her and Coyote through the final round of judging. In the hours leading up to the finals, we led them under the trees to graze and sat with them for hours, resting them both physically and mentally. While a couple of the trainers rode their horses, some for hours, we decided to rely on what we'd taught the horses in the months leading up to the competition, rather than drilling them into exhaustion.

With this in mind, we lay in the grass reflecting back over our journey and what we'd learnt from these special horses. While only two of ours had made it to the competition, all 11 Mustangs that had crossed our lives in the past three months had affected us in powerful ways. Tonight would be our last moments with Coyote and Jackie, and we wanted our final ride to be for fun, not to win. We didn't want or need the pressure or expectation to go well, which had the potential to lead to disappointment. Instead, we wanted to enjoy every minute, focus on the horses and enjoy ourselves as much as possible. We wanted to walk away with no regrets — which is a remarkable thing to be able to say in a competition environment; it means knowing that you haven't compromised the horse's welfare in any way and, more importantly, that you can look back and know that there is nothing you would have changed about the ride.

WALKING INTO THE ARENA ALONGSIDE THE OTHER finalists, in front of the crowd, was a daunting experience and nerves got the better of me. We'd made it into the top 10 and were now guaranteed an overall placing, so in some ways there was less pressure — but in other ways there were more expectations. Most of the horses in the top 10 were fairly evenly matched; everyone had a good shot of taking home the title, especially in a freestyle. It would come down to how they performed on the night. Even more importantly, potential owners were in the crowd, watching and judging the horses on the five-and-a-half minutes they would have in the arena. Knowing that you only had one chance to convince the crowd that your horse was special was overwhelming; luckily less so for me, since I was sure that Mark would end up with Jackie.

Alexa was third to go, producing a lovely and fairly accurate compulsory, and she exited the arena with a satisfied smile. Coyote was feeling good, and with just 20 minutes to prepare for her freestyle while the other trainers did their compulsory patterns, Alexa dismounted and rushed off to get changed while Vicki, Amanda, Kirsty and our mums prepared the horse, painting on a skull and crossbones and threading beads into her mane.

I was one of the last horses in the draw and was struggling in my warm-up: Jackie was tired and I wasn't mentally in the right frame of mind. One of the trainers rode up beside me and gave me a pep talk, and it was exactly what I needed to hear. Although he was riding just two horses before me, the time he gave me was hugely appreciated. I continued to warm up, with renewed focus, following his offered advice. By the time Jackie and I entered the arena, she was soft and supple. It didn't feel like we were riding in front of a crowd; it felt like we were riding at Jen's place on the arena. Jackie's focus was on me and she worked her best, accurately performing walk to canters, precise stops, roll-backs and effortless rein-backs, and she did everything on a soft contact. Pleased, I rode out of the arena with a huge smile, and it wasn't until I dismounted and ran our ride back through my mind that I realised I had missed out an entire move — I had side-passed left and done a spin, but had forgotten to side pass to the right before the second spin.

Another of the trainers had also missed a key move in the compulsories, and I headed over to find out how much it would affect us. Both of us would receive a score of zero for that part of the pattern, affecting our overall scores, but since each move was judged separately we still had a good chance of placing well. Shrugging, I put it from my mind. I might have stuffed up, but Jackie had been perfect and I was incredibly pleased with her. With Alexa about to re-enter the arena for her freestyle, I dismounted and hurried inside to watch.

Coyote looked like a seasoned schoolmistress, not fazed by the crowd, as she cantered into the arena with the tarpaulin flying, and she did a smooth and precise stop at the three-quarter mark. Like she'd practised, Alexa pulled the tarp up and over the horse, covering her completely, before re-mounting and riding off. From there she did spins and side passes, before dropping the anchor and doing a sliding stop before the rope pulled tight, and then holding a pirate flag while jumping over small uprights. To finish, a large exercise ball was thrown from the crowd for Alexa to catch, then she bounced it on the ground beside her before tossing it back up into the grandstand. Trotting to the bridge, she rode onto it and halted in the centre, where she turned around in the saddle

Top
Alexa and Coyote dragging
a tarpaulin in during their
freestyle final where they
placed second overall.

Middle
Jackie and I during
the overall prize-giving
where we placed sixth.

Bottom
The public interacting
with the horses before
they were auctioned.

until she was facing backwards, and rode out the gate waving to the crowd. Apart from one wrong canter lead, it had gone like clockwork and we were all pleased for Alexa and Coyote — they had done themselves proud.

Since Jackie was already warmed up from the compulsories, I only mounted a few minutes beforehand to familiarise her again with the flowing cape strung with helium balloons. Like in her compulsory pattern, Jackie worked beautifully in her freestyle, jumping an imposing wall, doing an intricate turn on the forehand on a raised object and trotting on the buckle while I waved a Silver Fern flag, as well as the more predictable moves. There were certainly moments of greenness, and it wasn't as flawless as she'd been in our final practices, but in general I couldn't fault her. It had been a great last ride, and I jumped off and gave her a hug while everyone quickly stripped us of our costumes so we could re-enter the arena just moments later for the final prize-giving and auction.

Jackie and I placed sixth overall, after losing significant points from that missed move, and to Alexa's delight she and Coyote finished as Reserve Champions, behind rider Willow Newcomb and Truffles, another beautifully produced Mustang and the only combination to cut cattle in their freestyle.

There were only seconds between the prize-giving and the first horse to be auctioned; by tradition the champion was first, followed by the rest of the horses in the order of their hip numbers. It was jarring to see the champion ridden to the centre of the arena while the price rose. With the support of the public, Willow had raised the funds to buy back her mare, and won the bid at US$6800. The next two horses sold for only a couple of hundred each, and then it was Jackie's turn. Riding her forward, I used the bidding time to showcase Jackie to the best of our ability; she'd sparked up with the atmosphere and wasn't feeling tired. Since all of the horses were lined up in the arena she was confident and happy — it had been tough for her to work alone in the arena for each of her classes. She trotted powerfully around the arena, performing flawless leg yields, side passes and rein-backs — in those final minutes she went better than on any of our other rides.

Since Mark's phone call, I'd come to terms with the thought of saying goodbye to Jackie. I'd come to America to save a Mustang and share her story, and I was confident that Mark was offering a home where she would thrive; I couldn't ask for more. As I rode her around, listening as the bidding rose, it was impossible not to enjoy the moment. Mark's bidder was on the phone, beating every bid offered, but others with big budgets had obviously come to the event hoping to take her home with them. When the bidding eventually stalled at US$7000, Mark was announced the winner and I felt at peace at last. It felt like the right home for her, and I hoped that she was everything he wanted and that he would be everything she deserved.

Prices for the remaining horses were low, the majority selling for between US$200 and US$1000. The longer the auction went on, the lower the prices became — when Coyote stepped forward, she only fetched US$1750 and we were speechless. She'd certainly been worth more, and we could only hope that she was going to a home that understood her. Amanda was worried, not knowing who had got the final bid — there was one person we definitely didn't want to walk away with one of our horses, and she was convinced that this person had bought Coyote. Amanda shared her concerns with us and, dreading the outcome, Alexa walked dejectedly back to the stables leading Coyote. It was awful not knowing who had bought your horse, and we strongly disagreed that auctioning the horses was in their best interests.

Unlike Amanda, I was sure I knew who Coyote's winning bidder was, and to the others' relief I was right — it was the same lady who was grazing our prison Mustangs for us! Rachel had placed the bid on her friend's behalf, and the young lady was excited to have Coyote join her family. Rachel was very horse-savvy, and spoke so highly of her friend that we were confident Coyote would have a good life. Less than an hour later, Alexa had to load Coyote onto a trailer and say goodbye; it was an emotional parting for all of us as we'd all become invested in the horse's journey.

Unlike Alexa, Kirsty and I had one more day with our mares, and we drove them back to Jen's so that they could unwind in the pasture.

Falling into bed that night we could barely form a sentence. It had been an exhausting week, filled with highs and lows, and we were just so thankful that it was over and — more importantly — that all three of our EMM mares had such wonderful homes.

On our last morning in America, we frantically finished packing, trying to decide what to take with us and what to leave behind. Our work with the Mustangs was by no means over, and all of us were determined to return and continue to raise awareness about the plight of these special horses. In the end, all of the horse gear — including our Western saddles and cowgirl hats — were stored in Jen's shed; we certainly wouldn't need any of it in New Zealand, and it seemed a waste of money to post it home to only send it back when we eventually returned.

While the others finished packing the car, Kirsty went with Digit to her new home and I ran down to the pasture to say a last goodbye to Jackie. As tears blurred my vision, I hopped on her bareback in a halter for one last canter across the field, and was again reminded just how much I had come to love this mare. Leaving her behind was one of the hardest things I've ever had to do.

Epilogue

Resting on our way to Cache Lake
in Yellowstone National Park.

Alexa and Tracey doubling on Coyote during our ride in Paintbrush Canyon in the Grand Teton National Park.

Since 2012 we have worked with over 40 wild horses, and each one has taught us something new. We are better horsewomen now than we were when we first began taming wild horses at just 20, 23 and 25 years of age, and undoubtedly we aren't as good now as we'll be in a year, or in 10 years. It seems like a lifetime ago that we first stumbled our way through the process of taming the initial 11 Kaimanawas, and we look back and see just how much we have learnt. We have always believed that every horse has something to teach us, and this was never more true than during our time in America.

After spending an intensive 100 days training and travelling with our Mustangs throughout the Wild West, they came to mean so much to us. Of all the horses Alexa, Kirsty and I have ever trained, our EMM Mustangs are the ones we take the most pride in. They learnt so much in their three months of ridden work, and were safer to ride on trails than any other horses we know. We could trust them completely, and we often used to say that if we were ever injured our Mustangs would carry us safely off the mountains.

In the arena they were equally progressive; Digit and Jackie were always soft, and willing to learn what was asked of them, and Coyote, too, reached this level of training in those final weeks. From leg yields through side passes and flying changes to jumping over a metre, they took everything in their stride, and had more advanced flat-work than any domestic horse we have worked with in the same amount of time — a remarkable achievement considering that most of our rides were on the buckle, trail-riding through National Parks. They did so well that Alexa and I got invited to take part in the Mustang Magic, a prestigious annual wild horse challenge — only 25 trainers worldwide are invited each year. Although we decided not to compete, as it would have meant returning to America just six weeks later and staying for another four months, it was a massive recognition of the work we had done.

For Vicki and Amanda, the horses they trained in America also came to mean a lot to them. Deacon and Gunnar will always hold a special place in their hearts because of their cheeky personalities and their ability to adapt so quickly to domestication. There are times when we regret turning them out after only two weeks' work; although this allowed us to save additional horses from the BLM yards, it also meant that we couldn't spend as much time with them as we wanted. If we'd been able to have 100 days of training with them I think they would have exceeded every expectation of a wild horse and been impossible to part with, so perhaps it's a blessing — saying goodbye after 14 days was hard enough. The family that rehomed Gunnar, also fell in love with Rayna, and together these two Mustangs, who came to mean so much to Vicki, will spend the coming years trail-riding through the mountains.

For Amanda, Bragg is a thrice-in-a-lifetime horse; alongside Showtym Viking and Showtym Cassanova, her two Grand Prix pinto showjumpers, he is her favourite. Amanda loves a horse that not only has the talent for top-level jumping but that she can also trust to hop on bareback in a halter and gallop around the hills without a care in the world — a horse always game for feral adventures. Unlike Jackie and me, whose journey together has come to an end, Amanda still retains ownership of Bragg, and he is in quarantine in preparation to fly to New Zealand.

Our other two prison geldings have found their forever homes: Parker with Rachel and her family (who also re-homed Deacon), and one of Jen's friends has taken Smith.

While each horse became something special in its own right, it was the Mustangs' overall persona that really captured our hearts. They had a way about them that was always so gentle, honest and open. They loved the adventures we offered them — after years of confinement in the BLM yards, their time with us was the closest to freedom they'd had since roaming wild with their herds in Oregon, Nevada and California.

Our Mustangs are only 11 of the 50,000 wild horses currently wasting away in government holding yards. The Mustang is one of America's greatest waste of assets, and we will do whatever is in our power to help solve this problem.

Top
Vicki and Rayna in Yellowstone National Park, the mare's fifth ride.

Bottom
Amanda couldn't bear to part with Bragg, her prison Mustang, and used
her prize money from the Olympic Cup to fly him home.

ACKNOWLEDGEMENTS

Thank you

As always, the adventures found in these pages wouldn't have been possible without the people who crossed our paths during our 100 days in America, nor the people who joined us from the beginning.

First and foremost, thank you to Alexa and Kirsty; you have worked alongside us with the horses for many years, but it was our time in America that turned you from friends to family. They say travelling with anyone is a true test of friendship — either it pulls you together or it tears you apart. I can honestly say the side of you both that we got to know during our adventures made us value you even more as people, respect you more than words can say and forge a lifelong friendship. Thank you for always being loyal, spontaneous, willing to rough it, and for smiling alongside us during both the good times and the bad.

Time and time again we were astounded by the generosity shown towards us during our time road-tripping through the Wild West. From these people we learnt that the term 'Cowboy Code' is not just a Wild West legend, it's a way of life for many and we have been inspired to integrate their level of kindness into our everyday lives.

To Matt, Stacie and your beautiful kids, you were the first people we knew in the States and you set the precedent for the generosity that would follow. Thank you for the use of your fantastic facilities and the always entertaining stories.

To the entire Emmett crew, especially Jen and her family, never have we met such kind, open people. You made us feel like family from the very first day and we can never thank you enough for the hospitality you showed both us and our many Mustangs. In you, we know we have found our own American family and look forward to our next adventures together.

To Liz and Bob at the NZ Ranch, thank you for inviting us to stay at your beautiful slice of Kiwiana in the middle of Oregon. We will be back to share more fantastic tales and five-star meals.

To the entire Parelli Family; Pat and Linda, for allowing us to well and truly over-stay our welcome at your Colorado ranch, we are beyond grateful for the hospitality you showed. Mark, the knowledge, honesty and wisdom you shared transformed us, both as entrepreneurs and in our approach to business. Every goal, concept and project we have accomplished since returning to New Zealand has been inspired by what we learnt in our short time with you. Caton, Whitney, Elle, Ryan and Rachel, thank you for the memories! To our knight in shining armour, Joseph, you rescued us more times than we care to count and we hope one day we can repay you somehow.

Ricky, you were a friend found in the most unlikely of places — thank you for taking the risk of letting five young girls on wild Mustangs help search for your cattle.

To Joshua Manning and your lovely family, you are kindred spirits and we know we will be seeing you again soon.

To the people in the Bureau of Land Management, and the Mustang Heritage Foundation and all our fellow Extreme Mustang Makeover trainers, every single one of you has a common trait: a fierce passion for America's Mustangs. Thank you for everything you do.

Most importantly, a huge thanks goes to our parents. We are incredibly fortunate you agreed to look after our 50 horses while we were out of the country for so many months . . . I don't think we will ever comprehend how much work and worry went on while we were away, and we are truly thankful that you not only support our dreams, but make it possible for us to pursue what we are truly passionate about. We consider ourselves lucky to be your daughters.